A *Confronting Fundamentalism* Book

Confronting Religious Denial of Gay Marriage
Confronting Religious Violence
Confronting Religious Judgmentalism
Confronting Religious Absolutism
The Confrontational Wit of Jesus
Confronting a Controlling God

CONFRONTING RELIGIOUS DENIAL OF SCIENCE

CONFRONTING RELIGIOUS DENIAL OF SCIENCE

CHRISTIAN HUMANISM AND THE MORAL IMAGINATION

CATHERINE M. WALLACE

 CASCADE *Books* · Eugene, Oregon

CONFRONTING RELIGIOUS DENIAL OF SCIENCE
Christian Humanism and the Moral Imagination

Confronting Fundamentalism

Cascade Books
An Imprint of Wipf and Stock Publishers
199 W. 8th Ave., Suite 3
Eugene, OR 97401

www.wipfandstock.com

PAPERBACK ISBN: 978-1-4982-2874-9
HARDCOVER ISBN: 978-1-4982-8853-8
EBOOK ISBN: 978-1-5326-0350-1

Cataloguing-in-Publication data:

Names: Wallace, Catherine M.

Title: Confronting religious denial of science : Christian humanism and the moral imagination / Catherine M. Wallace.

Description: Eugene, OR: Cascade Books, 2016 | Series: Confronting Fundamentalism | Includes bibliographical references and index.

Identifiers: ISBN 978-1-4982-2874-9 (paperback) | ISBN 978-1-4982-8853-8 (hardcover) | ISBN 978-1-5326-0350-1 (ebook)

Subjects: LCSH: 1. Religion and science. 2. Religion and science History. 3. Fundamentalism. I. Title.

Classification: BL 240.2 W275 2016 (print) | BL 240.2 (ebook)

Manufactured in the U.S.A.   JUNE 23, 2016

for Aislin Grace Wallace and Adelia Wren Wallace,
to whom the future belongs

Table of Contents

Preface

Thanks for picking up this book. After so many years of solitary work, it's thrilling to welcome a reader. I'm delighted you are here, and I hope you find what you are looking for. I look forward to hearing from you when you are finished reading. Contact me through my website, CatherineMWallace.com, through Twitter (@ Cate_Wallace) or through Facebook (Catherine M. Wallace Books). I'll do my best to reply promptly.

This book stand on its own, completely self-contained. But I have written six similar books, each focused on a different objection to hate-mongering, hard-Right Christian fundamentalism. In addition to being antiscience, this strain of Christianity is anti-gay. It's theocratic—the kind of thinking that was once responsible for crusades and inquisitions. It's absolutist. It's judgmental. It misrepresents Jesus because it misses his dark and confrontational wit. And, finally, it portrays God as an improbable and vindictive Old Man in the Sky. You can download a full introduction to this set of books from my author website, CatherineMWallace.com.

But simply *confronting* fundamentalism is not enough. We also need a strong, religiously neutral language for moral values shared by the vast majority of Americans. Each of my books demonstrates or exemplifies two concepts that I hope can become part of this shared conceptual language.

The first is *humanism*, which has two components. First and foremost, it is a personal moral commitment found in every global religious tradition: we must be *humane* to one another. Second, *humanism* is an intellectual commitment to critical thinking and the honest use of language.

As a movement, humanism began in the 1300s among poets and writers in "the humanities," from which the movement first took its name. Although some of them were clergy, and a few held very high posts in the church, for the most part these men were Christian public intellectuals. They were the very first to offer a distinctively modern critical engagement with the Bible and with the evolution of Christian belief in classical antiquity. They were also the first thinkers in the West to begin to recognize the extraordinary power of *cultural context*. Over time, as their work rippled through the culture, their influence evoked what we now call "the Renaissance."

Eight centuries later, however, "humanism" has acquired a much broader frame of reference. Today it names those who share a pragmatic, morally sensitive commitment to critical thinking and to the common good, with a strong emphasis on clear language and accurate information derived from the best available research. As a result, today there are Christian humanists, secular humanists, Buddhist humanists, Hindu humanists, Jewish humanists (secular and religious both), Muslim humanists, and so forth. "Humanism" has of course been vilified on the far Right as rabidly antireligious if not downright demonic. But humanism has never been opposed to *religion*. It is opposed to the *abuse* of religion. It is opposed to deliberate lies, to bigotry, to dishonest rhetoric, to the abuse of power, to reveling in the prospect of violence against others, and so forth.

My second useful concept is *moral imagination*. Imagination properly defined is the human cognitive ability to cope with paradox, to recognize patterns, and to think symbolically about a complex, polyvalent, dynamic reality. That's what Einstein was talking about when he said that imagination is more important than knowledge. The specifically *moral* imagination is this cognitive ability focused upon ethical questions. That's why each book in this series focused upon a moral failure of hard-Right, highly politicized Christian fundamentalism.

Point by point, issue by issue, each book in this collection will offer for your consideration some bit of wisdom provided by the specifically *Christian* moral imagination. That's not a covert "come to Jesus" plea. It's a plea to recognize that an immense cultural heritage is at risk no less decisively than statues of the Buddha blown up by the Taliban. I will offer insight that you don't have to become Christian to admire, just as you don't have to become Buddhist to admire Buddhist insight. To paraphrase the Dalai Lama, the point here is not becoming Christian. The point is to become wise.

And the wisdom we need most right now is the wisdom to reclaim the common ground that we share. We have gotten here from many directions, guided by many moral traditions. That diversity should be a source of strength and vitality, just as our ethnic diversity should be. It will be, it can be, if reasonable and informed people speak up. *And listen to one another.*

I'm honored by your willingness to listen to me. Thanks for being here.

Acknowledgements

In the decade I spent working on this book and others like it, I was repeatedly cheered on by generous audiences and critical readers. I owe a lot to these good people and to the local congregations or civic organizations that invited me to speak. These audiences read or listened patiently as I struggled to get my thinking in order and my sources under control. They patiently endured academic digressions that I later deleted. They convinced me that the world is full of open-minded, compassionate, morally sensitive people who delight in the quirky facts of cultural history.

Above all, they influenced my writing in quite remarkable ways. They insisted that stories are crucial and so I should tell more of them. One evening I worried aloud that the storytelling was distracting. Didn't it disrupt the flow of my argument?

"Look," one woman insisted sharply, "That's how I know it's an important point. You stop and tell a story." Everyone else nodded. Well, okay then. Stories. The more stories I told, the more often audiences told me that the stories were crucial.

Audiences also gave me permission to restate classical issues in philosophy or theology using very down-to-earth language. During discussion after my presentation, I'd reframe some complicated issue with an "it's like this" analogy. *Say that,* people would insist. *Just say that. Why didn't you just say that in the first place?* Let me tell you why: I was haunted by the Ghost of Professors Past, that's why. In time I banished that ghost (well, mostly). But I could never have done so without their flat-out and repeated insistence that they wanted to hear this more immediate, more vulnerable voice.

And that's not all. They convinced me I had to keep going. Their raw anger and bitter frustration kept me at my desk. I realized that there are a lot of us—Christian humanists and secular humanists alike—who sharply oppose the hard-Right, highly politicized misappropriation of Christianity. Lots of people are eager for the back story and the alternatives that I have to offer. They don't have the time to read all the stuff that I've read, and furthermore they don't have the scholarly background some of my sources presuppose. But they are just as curious and just as passionate as I am. They were as happy to find me as I've been to find a good plumber, or a competent tax guy, or a clever app. We need one another's skills.

In my audiences were Christians who are angry that the Christian "brand" has lost all connection to Jesus of Nazareth. They want their religion back. They want their God back. They are seriously pissed that "Christian" has come to mean "ignorant bigot," even though they understand that perception.

In my audience were scientists, engineers, and physicians. They argued fiercely that Christianity has an ignoble history of denying scientific facts and abusing scientists, a very serious topic I address more fully in *Confronting Religious Violence*. But they also complained bitterly about popular misunderstandings of science generally. That sent me off into a whole new branch of research; it had a huge impact on my final argument.

In my audiences were secular humanists. Some are outraged by encounters with "church people." Their stories haunt me. Some are outraged by the transparently anti-intellectual and theocratic ambitions of the radical Religious Right. They are offended by claims that this is a "Christian" nation and so one narrow version of Christianity should be allowed to usurp the law of the land and the democratic process. Many secular humanists are of course ex-Christians: some rejected that rigid, judgmental, hard-Right religiosity, which was the only version of Christianity available to them.

Others were religiously unaffiliated. Some had grown up unaffiliated. Others drifted away from dysfunctional congregations or from a faith that felt self-absorbed, irrelevantly dogmatic, and remote from the actual moral issues confounding daily life. Still others had tough and honest questions about the intellectual consistency of Christian beliefs or about Christian complicity in wrong-doing of one kind or another. Clergy or Sunday school teachers had dodged these questions. That was that, as far as they were concerned. I have to respect anyone who takes religion seriously enough to reject incoherent versions.

I was honored when those who are openly hostile to Christianity were nonetheless willing to listen to me. I was honored that they realized I'm not trying to convert anybody. They trusted me on that point. And they pushed hard, asking terrific questions and holding their ground when I pushed back. That process helped me clarify my thinking. It helped me understand my primary audience, which *is* secular humanists.

Some in my audiences have belonged to other faith traditions. These people were often quite eloquent about what they have found and why they value it. That too was invaluable. It helped me to find a conceptual language sufficiently open to communicate broadly.

Late in the process, I discovered major public affirmation of conversations like the ones I'd been having for ten years. In April 2014, the Brookings Institute issued a report, *Faith in Equality,* calling on Christian political progressives to reach out both to secular political progressives and to politically progressive religious conservatives for whom "Christianity" still has a clear theological connection to what Jesus actually taught about inclusivity, the image of God in everyone, and social justice as delineated by the great Jewish prophets. I take this report as evidence that the tide is turning nationally in opposition to hard-Right reactionaries in the Christian tradition.

I'm delighted to be part of that. I'm even more delighted to feel that I am speaking both to and for a solid core of ordinary, moderate, religiously tolerant Americans.

Grace and peace be with us all.

1

Confronting Fundamentalism: It's Antiscience

The problem at hand is in the news week after week: a hard-Right, highly politicized Christian fundamentalism has been repeatedly involved in a denial of science. Religious denial of evolution is merely the most famous example. And it persists: despite the fact that a federal judge declared that "creation science" is not biology, "creationists" on textbook committees in Texas continue to wreak havoc in the textbook market nationwide. That's a problem for more than biology teachers. Geology and astronomy also challenge the historical accuracy of Genesis. Science illiteracy, already widespread, threatens yet another generation.

Another example: climate change, widely accepted as indisputable fact elsewhere in the world, remains controversial in the US. And why? Some particularly radical Christians insist that it is "unbiblical" to think that the fate of the planet may rest in our hands, not in the hands of God. But the bigger problem is the extent of fundamentalist religious hostility to science in general. People who are already committed to a denial of science have proved a willing audience for lobbyists and others who seek short-term gain from blocking climate legislation.

Religious denial of science sows a host of problems. As a Christian, I am obligated to speak up on such issues, because Christian fundamentalism can only be stopped from within Christianity and in Christian terms. The illegitimacy of their claims needs to be clear to everyone, believers and nonbelievers alike, because that and that alone will deny them the religious credibility and the religious political cover that they seek.

That's what I intend to do.

What's at Stake Today

What's at stake in the religious denial of science is far more than willfully ignorant denial of solidly established research results. Far more than "facts" have been denied, distorted, or obfuscated. What is ultimately at stake is the proper and necessary relationship between Christianity and scientific research in a high-science, high-tech culture. If American culture were an organism, I'd say it has a broken leg, or possibly something far more serious—a malignancy, perhaps, perhaps the malfunction of a major perceptual capacity like sight or hearing.

This malfunction matters because problem solving in a high-tech democracy requires far more than scientific research and well-established findings. We also need virtue. For example, problem solving requires the social and political will to act in appropriate ways, with humble safeguards and with a modest, honest willingness to correct course as necessary along the way. Problem solving requires the moral courage and the moral resolve to do what is right even when it is difficult, costly, or inconvenient. Problem solving requires a capacity for paradox: deep responsibility to the common good must be matched by an equally deep responsibility to the rights of each individual. The needs of the present must be balanced with the needs of the future, despite how difficult that can be. Problem solving requires both the ability and the willingness to persuade others to go along, but persuasion in a democracy demands more than data sets. Persuasion requires poetry: images, analogies, storytelling that makes the issue at hand concrete enough and relevant enough to garner the necessarily broad consent.

Christianity, like other religions and like the best of ethical-secular humanism, has immense resources for inculcating virtue and for telling the stories that persuade people to take costly moral action to serve the common good. But Christian fundamentalism keeps coming down on the wrong side of issues, supporting willful ignorance, intransigent political extremism, and an irresponsible denial of the facts. I contend that Christian fundamentalist denial of science is a moral failure of considerable significance.

For scientists and nonscientists alike, and for thoughtful religious people in any faith tradition, the conflict between science and Christian fundamentalism is an appalling state of affairs. But the solution here is not to denounce Christianity across the board, hoping that if it were sufficiently denounced and widely enough ridiculed then it would simply disappear. That's magical thinking too. Worse yet, it is ceding to the Religious Right all of the cultural capital they have already misappropriated so successfully. The solution here, I propose, is a deeper understanding of the cultural currents that have swept us into this dangerous situation. We have to understand how we *got* here if we are going to find our way out.

In what follows, then, I will trace two misunderstandings that are deeply rooted in our shared cultural history. One is the popular image of "science" in our culture. The other is the popular understanding of metaphor. At first glance, the two issues might seem remarkably different. In fact they are remarkably interrelated. But for now, for the sake of a simple preliminary summary of my major themes, I'll discuss these problems one at a time.

Misunderstanding Science

Genuine, ordinary, experimental science has been attacked by a hard-Right, highly politicized religious fundamentalism. But it has also been attacked by another, far less visible cultural development: a wildly inappropriate demand for absolute beyond-all-question TRUTH. As a result, working scientists are hemmed in on both sides. On the one hand, biblical literalists won't listen to the facts of evolution, the facts of climate change, and so forth. But on the other hand, there is an equally unreasonable demand for a quality of certainty that science cannot provide. Such demands are not sat-isfied by modest, precisely delineated research results and compli-cated statistical probabilities. As a result, scientists are condemned for failing to provide the absolute TRUTH that people expect "sci-ence" to provide.

This is not pretty. Because the West has become such an in-tensely technological culture, widespread misunderstanding of sci-ence is quite nearly catastrophic. In effect, this distorted version of "science" has become something like *a fundamentalist religion* all of its own. Ordinary, empirical, experimental science has been recast as a source of absolutist, beyond-all-question TRUTH.

That's crazy. But it has happened, and we need a for label it. Let's call the distorted version "dogmatic scientism." That's not a perfect label, but I've been trying for months now to find a perfect label. This is the best I have found. In fact, I am increasingly fas-cinated by the fact that we don't have a familiar label for co-opted science. It's not pseudoscience: pseudoscience is people claiming that apricot pit enemas will cure your liver cancer, or crystals on a lanyard around your neck will cure your arthritis. Neither can I call it "science as a religion," because we can't go on assuming that "religion" means "absolutist-authoritarian nonsense." "Dogmatic scientism" is not a catchy phrase, I admit. But for now it will have to do.

Maybe some examples will help. Dogmatic scientism has co-opted authentic science whenever scientific findings are blithely ex-aggerated or erroneously extrapolated—and then scientists attacked for what they never said. (*Never* eat butter? They never said *never* eat butter. Cardiologists and endocrinologists and nutritionists doing empirical research on diet outcomes never advocated substituting partially-hydrogenated palm oil plus lots of sugar and extra salt and calling that "heart healthy.") Dogmatic scientism is trying to co-opt authentic science whenever politicians or policy makers demand a higher or more sweeping quality of certainty than what scientific evidence can ever provide—and then politicians ignore what the scientists *have* said because it's "just a theory." Dogmatic scientism generates expectations by patients that prognosis can be deter-mined by something equivalent to a tape measure, or that medical diagnosis and treatment ought to be as simple and unequivocally successful as replacing a gear in a mechanism—and if it's not, or it can't be, then physicians are attacked for "not knowing anything."

Popular misunderstandings of science frustrate honest, sophisticated scientists terribly, just as popular misunderstandings of Christianity frustrate sophisticated believers. In fact, I suspect that the most frustrated group out there is made up of people who are both working scientists and honest, sophisticated believers.

Misunderstanding Metaphor

Just as science has been widely misunderstood, so also metaphor has been widely misunderstood—and especially what it means to say that something is symbolic. For instance: because I do not read Genesis as a literal account of planet formation and human origins, I can be said to read those narratives "metaphorically." Just as Genesis does not trump biology and geology, so also the story of Jesus walking on the water does not trump physics and what physics attests about the surface tension of water. And so I can be said to read that account "metaphorically" as well. But for many people, that means I think those stories are false, or trivial, or to be brushed aside. And because I read those stories "metaphorically" rather than literally—that is, not as accounts of actual historical events—I look like a liberal theologian of a kind that was quite common in the first half of the 1900s.

I am not a liberal theologian. I am not a theologian at all, for a start, or at least not in any formal academic sense: I am a literary critic and a cultural historian. That's a different expertise. But in particular, I can't be lumped in with "liberal theologians" because I radically disagree with how they read Scripture.

Liberal theology at its worst regards biblical narratives as something like quaint illustrations of systematic theology. A narrative could be reduced to the philosophical claim that it embodied— the moral of the story, so to speak—and then the story discarded, as the shell of a walnut is discarded after we extract the edible part. (Never mind "walking on water." The moral of the story is that we need to trust Jesus.) It is as if the master poets and storytellers of the world's single most influential book would have written propositional systematic theology if only they knew how. But they didn't know how to say, "what matters is trusting Jesus." So they told stories instead.

For liberal theology, the essence of the faith is this set of abstract ideas. For liberal theologians, miracle narratives are almost embarrassing. They are not to be taken *seriously*. What's "serious" is the moral of the story—a moral that is far more clearly delineated by centuries of creedal orthodoxy and abstract academic theology. That's how theology displaces poetry and storytelling.

As a literary critic, I find that appalling. It's as naive to translate narratives into propositions as it to believe that the earth was created in six days ten thousand years ago. Underneath such misreading is the belief that "metaphor" means "false." Such beliefs date from the late 1500s and early 1600s, when metaphor was regarded as merely decorative—and furthermore deceptively so. Dishonestly so. But linguists today argue that metaphor is essential to language, to cognition, and to critical thinking. Metaphor is both a cognitive strategy (the ability to think by analogy) and a semantic resource (the linguistic ability to stabilize and examine paradox). But in the eyes of many people, to say that a statement is "metaphoric" is to say that it is something close to "fake." To say "just a metaphor" in dismissive tones is akin to saying "just an electron" and thereby brushing aside all of quantum physics.

For example, in my upcoming analysis of miracle narratives, I will argue that these miracles are profoundly symbolic actions, dense with allusion to other equally symbolic narratives elsewhere in Scripture. In saying that, I am not saying that these stories are false. I am not saying that Christianity is false. I am saying that Christianity is remarkably, powerfully *true,* but the truth that it offers is just a tad more sophisticated than believing that Jesus could change the surface tension of water. Furthermore, the truth that Christianity offers cannot be extracted from the Gospel narratives as a walnut is extracted from its shell. Doctrine and dogma and creed will never replace Scripture. Neither will musicology replace music, or literary theory replace literature, or art theory replace art.

The intellectually embarrassed liberal-theological effort to extract "Christianity" from the metaphoric and symbolic density of the Bible was a mistake. It arose in the very same decades where we find non-science intellectuals boldly asserting that dogmatic scientism is the new "religion of man." The co-opting of science and the theological misunderstanding of metaphor and narrative are two different but closely related aspects of Western culture after 1870 or so.

We can't straighten out the relationship between Christianity and science without first getting straight the misappropriation of "science" in Western culture. That's our first task together here. Our second task is to look plainly at miracles and at prayer as premier instances—supposedly—of magical thinking on the part of believers. And somewhere in the middle, between one task and the next, I'll turn to the anthropologist Clifford Geertz and the evolutionary psychologist David Sloan Wilson: Geertz argues that religions are systems of symbols creating a world view; Wilson argues further that the world view thus created is designed to minimize social conflict and encourage pro-social collaboration.

That works for me. It's minimalist, I grant: my faith is much more than a symbolic organization of my pro-social tendencies. But it's a solid starting point, and better yet it's one that makes sense to non-Christians. I contend that we need Christianity as one way of doing what Geertz and Wilson describe. We need that just as we need scientific research as a method for investigating the world around us. Both authentic Christianity and authentic science are remarkable powerful forces in American culture. They need to be understood clearly and their resources deployed honestly.

That's a basis upon which secular humanists, the religiously unaffiliated, members of other traditions, and Christian humanists can all acknowledge one another and collaborate intelligently. It is a basis upon which Christians and Hindus and Muslims and Jews and secularists—and anybody else out there—can minimize conflict and collaborate thoughtfully to serve the common good of the entire society. *Our* entire society, the colorful and glorious diversity of this remarkable nation. Together, collaboratively, we can confront religiously based radicalism, reclaim "moderate" and "compromise" and "expert" as honorable qualities, and then begin to solve urgent problems on the basis of the best information available.

Overview

I will begin, as always with a story: we need to keep the issues rooted in our own ordinary experience. My story of grappling with religion versus science issues will be chapter 2.

In chapter 3, I'll begin by going back to the Victorians. As I explain in *Confronting Religious Absolutism* [forthcoming], contemporary Christian fundamentalism has its origins in two mid-Victorian developments, papal infallibility and biblical inerrancy. Here I want to examine in detail something else that happened at the same point: science was culturally co-opted. It was co-opted as a remedy for the same cultural anxieties that lay behind the co-opting of Christianity.

That story continues in chapter 4. In the early decades of the 1900s, legitimate science was increasingly displaced in popular culture by dogmatic scientism, which was widely celebrated as a new-and-improved religion for a new century. Dogmatic scientism became an absolutist opponent to absolutist religious fundamentalism, which was gathering steam rapidly. Dogmatic scientism proclaimed the "secularization thesis" that religion is intellectually and culturally "primitive" and thus doomed to die out. The secularization thesis was social science orthodoxy for most of the twentieth century. That orthodoxy was mistaken. Nonetheless, it's vitally important to understand—and to respect—the rise of secularism. So I'll take some time to do so.

In chapter 5 I ask a fairly obvious question. Somewhere between Edward Tylor's *Primitive Culture* (1871) and Walter Lippmann's *A Preface to Morals* (1929), dogmatic scientism became for many the new and improved dogmatic religion. But what sort of religion is it? What is its implicit "theology"? The implicit theology of dogmatic scientism portrays scientific law as supreme, as divine, as in fact identical with God the Engineer Almighty. *That divine engineer at his keyboard is also the God imagined by religious fundamentalism.*

The Engineer Almighty is a divinity with serious problems. If this character has all of reality under his detailed control, then he has a lot to account for. Why is the world so fraught with pain and suffering?

Furthermore: the rise of such a theology demonstrates the extent to which our ideas about God are culturally constructed. They reflect our world view. And so the cultural history of how we think about "who God is" matters even for nonbelievers. It matters because speculation about the nature of God provides the cultural source code whereby we think and talk about who *we* are. "What God demands" similarly codes for what we demand of one another. Whether or not you think about human identity and our socio-moral obligations to one another using "God-talk" at all, the fact remains that God-talk is the ancient Western source code for such issues. That was for me a key recognition in trying to sort through the odd convergence between Christian fundamentalism and weirdly dogmatic popular misunderstanding of science.

Dogmatic scientism was not the only cultural alternative to fundamentalist versions of Christianity. There were a whole array of others in those crucial decades from 1871 to 1929. Some of them turned into that curse of the twentieth century, political totalitarianism. Totalitarianism is simply a secular form of theocracy: the state enforces an ideological "orthodoxy," murderously if necessary; ideological orthodoxy in turn undergirds and legitimates state authority. That's why totalitarianism—whether secular or religious— is such a threat to our collective well-being. What all totalitarian systems have in common is this: they have a Truth that cannot be questioned, and they seek control of the state in order to coerce obedience from the rest of us.

And so, if Christianity is not a particularly irrational variety of totalitarianism, *what is it?* Chapter 5 concludes with Clifford Geertz, who argues that religion is a system of symbols that generates a world view. I agree with that—and furthermore, symbolism is one of the most sophisticated cognitive tools that we have. (For more on symbolism, see *Confronting Religious Absolutism* [forthcoming], chapters 11 and 12.)

Chapter 6 continues exploring this idea. David Sloan Wilson, an evolutionary psychologist, builds on Geertz's claim. Wilson contends that the function of a religious system of symbols is to elicit and sustain pro-social behavior, including self-sacrifice and costly collaboration for the common good.

But here's an obvious consideration: symbolism is a strategy of meaning specific to the arts. Nothing is symbolic in and of itself. Religious symbolism is thus inextricably embedded in religious storytelling, song, visual arts, and dramatic performance. We need to grapple with religion *as an art,* not as a rival account of human evolution, geological history, and the like. We need to respect the truth-claims of its symbolism without turning symbolic narratives into dubious accounts of supposedly empirical observations.

In chapter 7 I begin to test the claim that Christianity can be understood as a system of symbols encouraging pro-social attitudes and behavior. I will describe miracles stories as narrative accounts of symbolic actions. (Scholars explain that all miracles stories in the ancient world were symbolic in this way.) In chapter 8 I'll tell one of my stories, this time about a playground confrontation over the nature of prayer. Chapter 9 will define prayer as an introspective creative process, not a call to divine tech support. In chapter 10 I'll take a look at neuroscience research into a prayer practice now secularized as "mindfulness based stress reduction" (MBSR). In chapters 11 and 12 I'll explain how prayer in the Christian tradition tries to go beyond what MBSR offers any of us. I am not trying to convince anyone to pray. But I am trying to convince everyone that prayer is not magical thinking.

But first, as always, a story: somebody I knew said she would be "praying for me," and I struggled to make sense of what she was saying. In some ways, it was embarrassing nonsense. But in other ways . . .

2

1971: The Novena

"Your mom tells me you are going to graduate school for a doctorate," she had written. "Congratulations! I'll make a novena to St. Jude for your success and happiness in your chosen field. Sincerely, Marge O'Malley."

A novena: nine days of prayers. To Saint Jude, the patron saint of hopeless causes.

I called my mother.

"Margaret O'Malley is an idiot. That woman prays to Saint Jude for everything! Ignore her."

I knew better than to push when Mom took that tone of voice. I also knew that Mrs. O'Malley was not an idiot. Not by a long shot.

Ignore the note? If only I could! It had set loose swarms of issues that I fervently wished to ignore. I didn't go to church; I didn't believe in the intercession of the saints or the power of novenas. But neither could I deny the baffling complexity of my response. I was baffled in so many different directions simultaneously that I didn't know where to turn.

Perhaps I should begin by explaining that in traditional Roman Catholicism, there are saints assigned to just about any problem you can imagine. Mid-century American Catholic piety was keen on that specificity. There were thick books of saints' lives to scour for the patron saint of drunken husbands, wayward children, leaky roofs, pending biopsies. There were religious goods stores selling small plastic statues of particularly popular saints: you could put your favorite on your kitchen windowsill, or maybe set him on your dresser with a small candle.

Mom pointedly disapproved of all that. Prayers were prayers. Too much attention to saints bordered on superstition. Nonetheless, in praying to the patron saint of hopeless causes for my academic success, Mrs. O'Malley may have crossed a line that even my mother took seriously.

Some of these saints were actual historical figures—the patron saint of bridges, for instance, died falling from a bridge; the patron saint of bear-keepers was mauled to death by a bear. Their demise translated into their patronal status: here is someone who understands your problem. Sometimes the linkage was more by tradition than history: how did St. Joseph become the patron saint of selling your home? That has never been clear to me, although I could concoct an explanation. (And when we were trying to sell our first house, Mom did insist that I had to bury a statue of St. Joseph upside down, in a small plastic bag to keep him clean, facing the house.)

Other saints are relics of the long stretch of centuries in which minor local deities were adopted wholesale into the Catholic church. They were transformed into "saints" and thence resumed their familiar duties as the patrons of this or that human endeavor, predicament, or locale. As the nuns had explained when I was in high school, the concept of "patron saints" allowed local worship traditions among the peasantry to pick up and carry on seamlessly even after the Roman Empire officially converted to Christianity (a development I discuss in *Confronting Religious Violence*, chapters 5–8).

With the vast influx of European immigrants to the US in the 1800s, these same habits of mind flowed directly into the immigrant experience of big-city governance. For instance, if you need something done in Chicago, don't call the mayor's office. Call your alderman. And in my working-class Irish-Catholic church, saints functioned as the aldermen of God. Don't bother the Big Guy. Talk to the right saint.

Better yet, maybe, skip the saint. Talk to the Virgin. Get to the Jewish mother of the Big Guy, and she will take it from there. Do you remember how Jesus caved when his mother demanded more wine at the wedding at Cana? That's the woman you need.

Not that Irish mothers are slackers, of course. When my mother had a need that God the Father Almighty seemed unlikely to understand, or too exalted to notice, she prayed to her own mother, the saintly Catherine Murphy. Once Grandma Murphy would have been at the door in a blink, ready to help with the chaos at hand. My mother's faith in her own mother was unshaken by the mere fact of death. Grandma Murphy was a comfort, dead or alive.

I could easily imagine Grandma Murphy sitting down for a good cuppa tea with the equally round, equally gray-haired Virgin Mary: the sisterhood of powerful older women, celestial style. Why bother with the likes of Saint Jude when you can pray to your own mother? Folk tradition from Mexico to China would agree with my Mom 100 percent.

Sociologists explain that Christianity swept the West in part because it combined both the pomp-and-circumstance pageantry of "temple" religion with the intimacy and immediacy of "personal" religion. Or to shift to a more familiar vocabulary, Christianity became both "religious" and "spiritual" simultaneously. On the one hand, it provided massive cathedrals with a royal priesthood and an array of ceremonies directly or indirectly affirming the cosmic legitimacy of the powers that be. On the other hand, it offered this colorful array of local saints and folk traditions to help ordinary people to maintain both their personal resilience and their local communities despite all the suffering to which flesh is heir. Public ritual plus grassroots allegiance is a potent mix even now.

Nor did the process of assimilation stop with reclaiming folk-gods as folk-saints. Festivals were "christened" as well. For instance, the Roman midwinter Saturnalia became Christmas. For ten days, beginning roughly December 21, we party nonstop—as if to convince the sun to return. The Puritans, that cheerful lot, forbade the observing of Christmas because they saw that it was an essentially pagan holiday with no legitimate basis in Scripture.

My favorite part of all this is the story behind Christmas trees. In December we set up trees in our living rooms, festooning them with lights and ornaments. Why? Because northern Europeans worshipped trees. Their midwinter folk traditions were also christened—and hence, the "Christmas" tree.

"Yule logs" have roughly the same origin: entire trees were dragged inside to be progressively burned during the week or so following the winter solstice. That's why a wood fire is still a standard part of our holiday iconography, even though setting the fireplace ablaze is a terrible idea if there's a decorated tree jammed into a corner, wrapping paper strewn across the floor, overexcited children toddling about, dinner guests standing in every spare foot of space, and the kitchen stove going full blast. Yule logs in the fireplace also generated yule log cakes, thickly and artfully frosted to look like tree bark. Merry Christmas, everyone: a high-calorie Saturnalian feast, a yule log fire, and a Christmas tree. Christianity is rich in such folk-tradition remnants: 2,000 years is a very long time.

Although the persistence of these folk customs fascinated me historically, it drove me crazy personally: I didn't live in the Middle Ages. Or I didn't want to live in the Middle Ages, which is where the religion of my childhood seemed to be stuck. Philosophically, scientifically, all too much of it struck me as nonsense. It was colorful; it was comforting in its familiarity (and don't forget "Christmas cookies"). But did I believe any of it? In Robert Coles's lovely phrase, I was a spiritually embarrassed agnostic intellectual. Emphasis on *embarrassed*.

After listening to my mother for a few minutes, I hung up the phone and returned to staring at the note. Saint Jude, the patron saint of hopeless causes. And Mrs. O'Malley, mother of nine or ten. The first two were older than I, and so they were probably out of college by now. If they had gone at all. Going to college wasn't unheard of in our neighborhood, but neither was it commonplace. Were the O'Malley's college types? Hard to say. If Mr. O'Malley were in a skilled trade—wasn't he a plumber?—sons almost always moved into apprenticeships. No matter what the older O'Malley kids were doing, I'd guess Mrs. O'Malley still had a kitchen full of kids at home. She was a busy woman.

But she would be taking ten or twenty minutes every day for nine days to sit quietly and pray for my success and happiness in my field. And what was I to make of that? She might go to church to pray. That was traditional but by no means required. Either on the first day or the last day she might go to church and light a candle— small pillars maybe two or three times the size of tea lights. They sat inside small glass cups arrayed in rows in a wrought-iron frame. The frame was set below a statue of the Virgin Mary and in front of a small altar set to one side of the main altar. When I was young, every Catholic church had these candles, although since then they have largely disappeared. Fire insurance, Mom said.

Whether from home or in church, with or without candles, a novena was a confrontation with God about something seriously wrong, deeply desired, or desperately needed. And to my unspeakable amazement, Mrs. O'Malley was taking time to do one for me.

To Jude, patron saint of hopeless causes. Was the neighborhood going to see my ambition as hopeless? As an obvious catastrophe in the making? Was Mrs. O'Malley herself outraged by my daring? A college degree for a woman was a quite sufficient challenge to the mores of our working-class world: my father's eldest sister had reamed him out for letting my sister and me go to college in the first place. Had I triggered some trip wire in Mrs. O'Malley's soul? Is that what prompted her note? I had never stopped to consider what the folks at church would think of my professional plans.

On the other hand, precisely because a novena was so serious, Mrs. O'Malley might have meant exactly what she said. I had to consider that possibility too. After all, it would be sinful to pray for someone's failure or their unhappiness. It was unthinkable to pray sarcastically, meaning the opposite of what you said. It would be blasphemy even to claim falsely that you would offer such a novena, no matter how offended you were. The rules about such matters were perfectly clear: legitimate prayers could be offered only for the right reasons and with the right intentions. The more I tried to figure this out, the clearer it seemed that she had to have meant what she said, without any shadow of irony—Saint Jude notwithstanding.

Perhaps Mrs. O'Malley was passionately on my side, passionately enough to signal that to me at a distance, in a time- and energy-consuming way that warms my heart even now. Got your back, kid. Go for it. What did my ambitions mean to her that she made this effort to support me?

Reluctantly I remembered Mom's and Dad's responses when I'd told them—just recently—about my plan to get a PhD.

Mom had been dumbfounded and angry. She argued fiercely that I should instead get a position in the typing pool at Standard Oil, where she worked. She might be able to help me get an interview, and surely as an English major I could probably type with reasonable speed. If I worked hard, I might be able to compete for a position as an executive secretary. Mom had moved from being an executive secretary to being an executive herself: surely I could too, despite not knowing a thing about business. I could learn. If I was as smart as they said, I could learn by paying attention to the documents I was set to typing. I could work my way up if I worked hard—and if I behaved myself. Here Mom gave me a look that I've known all my life.

Dad had confronted me on the front porch, quietly disagreeing with Mom. He thought I should be a stewardess. Not the typing pool but travel. See the world before I settled down to raise a family. Maybe the other stewardesses could teach me how to wear make-up? And how to dress? He was kindly but clear: if I needed more schooling at all, it would be to acquire a more traditional femininity. Enough of this jeans and turtlenecks business.

My parents were agreed on one thing: an opposition as unrelenting as my determination. I was their child, after all. And I was no longer a child.

On Sunday afternoon, Dad confronted me again in the hallway as I headed up the stairs to pack.

"Don't come home weird," he warned. My oldest brother had been home for a weekend recently from Boston, where he was working on his PhD in Semitic linguistics at Harvard. He had brought along some books to read—three books in three different languages, none of them English. He had set these books on the stairs going up to the bedrooms.

"I couldn't even read the titles," Dad complained, gesturing at the stair. And he repeated: "Don't come home weird." In the dim light, I could hardly see the expression on his face. And then he half-turned, looking away from me down the hall toward the den.

I would come home weird. I think we both knew that. Perhaps it was already too late. Was he holding back the urge to take me in his arms, resting his chin as always on the top of my head? Or was that what I wanted him to do? Both of us stood there, silent, until he turned and walked into the dining room. I went up to my room to finish packing. As I folded my jeans into my suitcase I felt as if I were heading over Niagara Falls in a barrel.

Hopeless causes indeed. The opening lines of a prayer I'd first learned in Latin surfaced in my mind unbidden: "Remember, oh most gracious Virgin Mary, that never was it known, that anyone who fled to thy protection, implored thy help, or sought thy intercession, was left unaided . . ."

So what had prompted this note from Mrs. O'Malley? Whose side was she on? Obviously Mom had told Mrs. O'Malley about my plans. And if Mom told one of her friends, Mom probably told dozens: in those days my mother had more friends than anyone you have ever met. An extraordinary extravert, she had a gift for making friends. Was she ranting to them about my stubborn foolishness? Or trying to brag about her daughter going for a PhD? I had no idea. I could imagine it either way. Or both at once: my mother was fully capable of conveying both messages simultaneously.

And if I knew my mother, she was also praying frantically about my foolishness to Grandma Murphy, for whom I was named. Surely that was part of my problem with Mrs. O'Malley's novena. Was I to imagine Grandma Murphy and Saint Jude going toe-to-toe up there? Even to ask that question is to imagine that God is a politician to be lobbied. Or perhaps a vending machine: who had the bigger stack of quarters, Mom or Mrs. O'Malley? I cringed. I wanted nothing to do with any of this.

Worse yet, I worried that I was in fact a hopeless cause. If I'd been of a mind to pray a novena about graduate school, Saint Jude might have been my first choice. Suddenly I wondered: did Mrs. O'Malley's prayers to Jude signal how clearly she understood what I was up against? Did she have frustrated ambitions of her own? Somehow I'd never stop to ask that about any of the women in the neighborhood. Such an obvious failure of my own imagination left me feeling even more intimidated.

⁓

I was also afraid that prayer actually did mean something, even though the usual ways of talking about prayer were philosophically shabby and scientifically nonsense. But the inadequacy of the usual explanations did not mean that prayer itself is necessarily nonsense. I prided myself on that quality of intellectual rigor. It held me captive amidst the buzzing swarm of my own ambivalence.

The fact remained that I could feel a power in Mrs. O'Malley's offer, a power that went far beyond her offering a gesture of emotional support in the face of my parents' fears and their incomprehension. She could have sent a simple friendly note: oh I heard, oh congratulations, oh I'm sure you will do well, oh I'm so proud of you. Any of that. All of it.

Instead she was praying a novena. She was offering moral support. Whether or not I believed in God, she did; and so what she was saying had a very different heft than ordinary social support. She was saying what I know the nuns in my high school would have said: I was morally accountable before God to develop my talents to the fullest extent possible and then to use those talents as richly as I could. That didn't mean it would be easy: I needed to pray. Or I needed someone like Mrs. O'Malley to pray on my behalf. Perhaps it felt like a hopeless cause for a working-class girl like me to go for a PhD, but the nuns would have said I needed faith strong enough to dream even the most hopeless dreams. The nuns would have wondered whether God was calling me to do this—and if I was being called, then God help me if I didn't listen. Mrs. O'Malley's novena was clearly her vote that God was indeed calling me to such unheard-of ambition.

One is supposed to pray fiercely and attentively about such calls, because the temptation to self-deception is so massive. But I had not prayed. I didn't believe in prayer. I didn't believe in God or God's "call." But for days I was haunted by images of Mrs. O'Malley pulling up alongside the church, where she could park in the shade, before ducking in the door for twenty minutes of silent, focused prayer. For my happiness and success in my chosen field, and to the patron saint of hopeless causes. To whom she turned for everything, Mom said. But why?

In 1971, I lacked both the courage and the personal maturity to pursue these unfocused intuitions that something here actually did make sense.

I also didn't know enough of what anyone would need to know in order to explore such questions coherently. In those days, I could not have begun to explain my much later recognition that prayer is a symbolic gesture. It's a symbolic action—a metaphor acted out. "I'll pray for you" is not necessarily an effort to manipulate the causal structure of the universe. Many believers speak as if it is, but that's because they are speaking casually, within the folk traditions of "personal religion" or what we now call "spirituality." They are not speaking with the scrupulous precision of philosophers.

But if you ask the honest Mrs. O'Malleys of the world whether their prayers are meant to elicit a change in the causal structures of reality, many of them will recoil in dismay. They know the difference between magic and religion, whether or not they can explain it clearly. They are not praying as an exercise in magical causality. They are praying because that is what one does in the face of life's difficulties and its desires. Christians pray just as Buddhists meditate: it's a spiritual practice that, sustained over time, reshapes the experience of life in certain fairly predictable ways toward greater resilience, lessened anxiety, greater compassion, clearer mental focus, and so forth.

There is a difference, then, between the philosophical naiveté of non-rigorous, philosophically untrained working-class believers and literal-minded claims that "with prayer, all things are possible" or that we need only ask our Heavenly Father and we shall receive whatever we want. That's not what Mrs. O'Malley's novena was about. She was not praying to a vending machine God.

But I had no idea how to grapple with what her novena did mean. And I never did forget what she had written. Something here does need explaining. And whatever it is, does it shed any light on the miracles attributed to Jesus in the Gospels? Really now, those miracles make one novena feel like small potatoes—except, of course, that the novena happened to me, so to speak.

Postscript

My parents and I never talked again about graduate school. They never asked whether I was happy or successful. Not a word, a silence that rippled out further and further as the years passed. But neither was there ever again the least hint of opposition from them. Not a hint. We had clashed, then we had hardly spoken for an entire year, and then they had backed down. And not just backed down: later they refinanced their mortgage, unexpectedly and without explanation paying off my undergraduate loans.

Maybe I was wrong but I was *theirs*, theirs in far more ways than any of us understood at the time.

3

Tylor, Frazer, and the Rise of Dogmatic Scientism

The conflict between Christianity and science today has its roots in Victorian panic at the erosion of absolute unquestionable external authority. Beginning in 1776—if not 1688—absolute monarchs became steadily less absolute; over the span of the 1800s, Western democracy began its slow ascent. In the 1700s, philosophy began with growing confidence to assert that "objective observation" is far less simple and far less reliable than it seems. That too was profoundly disconcerting. Christian biblical scholars began assembling evidence that the Gospels are not eyewitness accounts, that Moses himself did not write the book of Genesis, and so forth. Here was yet another loss of objective authority. Meanwhile, the Industrial Revolution and the rise of a new mercantile middle class was steadily eroding the traditional economic power and social status of the landed nobility, whose lands no longer yielded income equal to the lifestyle to which they were accustomed. As A. N. Wilson explains in *God's Funeral* (1999), these developments elicited something like a collective nervous breakdown among the Victorians. George Pattison makes much the same point in *Anxious Angels* (1999).

To remedy that anxiety, there were strong but unworkable counterclaims of absolute authority. In 1870, the pope had himself declared infallible. In the 1870s and 1880s, certain Protestants declared that the Bible is also infallible. According to them, the Bible is literally true both in its every statement about God or Jesus and at the factual level in its claims about planet formation, biology, human origins, subsequent historical events (including Noah's flood), and so forth. As I explain in more detail in *Confronting Religious Absolutism* [forthcoming], chapters 4 and 5, these infallibility claims are rooted in Europe's horrific religious wars between 1524 and 1660.

In this chapter I want to pick up that historical narrative. Just as Christianity was co-opted by these literal-minded assertions of religious authority, so also the nascent enterprise of empirical science was co-opted. It was co-opted along the same lines that had more or less co-opted Newton in the later 1600s: the culture was desperate for some rock-solid source of authority and truth. In the 1800s, as the same cultural anxieties intensified even further, there arose a more concerted effort to proclaim that "science" is One True Religion. In the 1800s as in the late 1600s, the people most responsible for such claims were neither scientists nor mathematicians. That's the story I want to tell.

The Victorian Sir Edward Tylor had no university degree at all, although on the basis of his work he was named the very first Professor of Anthropology at Oxford University. His far more famous student, Sir James Frazer, had a degree in classics, although he too is now accorded "founding father" status in anthropology. Both men are widely credited with initiating the "scientific" study of religion, even though there was nothing remotely "scientific" about their work. Given their status and their popularity in their own day, however, the conclusions reached by Tylor and by Frazer have achieved folklore status. Or perhaps their conclusions are more like urban legends: widely believed to be true but utterly false.

Today's conflict between "religion" and "science" derives from the clash between inerrant-infallible-fundamentalist Christianity and these equally erroneous, untenable Victorian claims about "science." That explains a lot. Or so it seems to me. I hope I can persuade you. Let's begin with a closer look at Tylor and Frazer.

Edward Tylor: Religion as Failed Science

Sir Edward Tylor of Oxford University was among the first to argue in a sustained way that religion is nothing more than crude pre-scientific thinking. Tylor's *Primitive Culture* (1871) argues that the essence of religion is the human philosophical desire to explain why reality is as it is. He claims that religion originates in something like the speculation of a primordial philosopher who tried to explain what's what and why.

Originally, Tylor argues, this primordial philosopher argued that there's a spirit inside every tree or stream or wolf. That's animism. Animism gave way to polytheism when migratory hunter-gatherer groups settled down into the first steeply hierarchical agricultural civilizations. Each large domain of the natural world was ruled by a particular god, just as each kingdom has its king. There's not a unique spirit in every sparrow flying past. Instead, there's a sea god, a river god, a god of grain, a god of cattle, a god of wine, and so forth. And that explains why things are the way they are.

With the rise of empires, he continued, polytheism gave way to monotheism: one god controls all of reality just as international emperors such as Nebuchadnezzar or Alexander the Great governed "the known world." The choices or desires of this "supreme god" explain why things are as they are.

But in the modern world, Tylor explained, we have science to explain to us why the world is as it is. The gods are simply outmoded explanations or disproved hypotheses. They have been displaced by rational scientific principles such as gravity or evolution or plate tectonics.

Shadows of Tylor still fall across the pages of science books for children in those introductory passages blithely explaining that earthquakes were once thought to be the work of angry gods—but now we know better. It's not the gods, it's simply plate tectonics. The divinities of old were simply obsolete efforts at scientific explanation. The same shadow falls across storybooks of classical mythology. It's easy to grow up assuming that these narratives were never anything other than "primitive" efforts at scientific explanation, and thence to assume that the sacred Scriptures revered by Christians (or Muslins, or Hindus) are simply more of the same. That's the influence of Tylor.

And that's a stunning misreading of sacred Scriptures in any tradition. It's also a stunning misrepresentation of what religions are trying to "do." It misunderstands the goals and objectives of Christianity, which is not to explain the causal regularities of the material world.

That's not the only problem with Tylor's work. As subsequent generations of anthropologists attest, the cultural record does not support Tylor's claim that religions universally evolve toward monotheism, nor that monotheisms arose universally whenever political empires conquered culturally diverse populations. Nor is there empirical evidence in the historical and cultural record that religion has always been primarily focused on explaining causal regularities in the material world. Religions might presuppose that the world makes sense—that things commonly happen for intelligible reasons—but that's a different matter. By comparison: poets writing about thunderstorms might presuppose in accordance with local culture that thunderstorms are an intelligible event, but that does not mean poets are trying to account for thunderstorms in a manner parallel to (or in competition with) meteorologists.

Nonetheless, Tylor's work did successfully provide a misleading basis upon which later thinkers have continued to claim that "science" has rendered "religion" obsolete as an explanation of the material world. And a generation later, one of Tylor's students took this misunderstanding even further into the murk.

James Frazer: Religion Is Magical Thinking

In 1891, twenty years after *Primitive Culture* was published, the classicist Sir James Frazer began publishing a series of studies building upon Tylor's work. *The Golden Bough*, which appeared by installments over twenty-five years, was immensely influential. I've seen some of Frazer's particular claims repeated as fact by people who either don't know the origins of the claim, or who fail to understand that his interpretations have been repudiated by anthropologists and historians who *are* attempting a "scientific" study of religion. In graduate school, I was sent to read around in *The Golden Bough* because of its influence on certain poets—with no warning at all that Frazer's analyses are nonsense.

Frazer argues that religion originates not in the purely scientific yearning to understand the world around us, as Tylor had suggested, but rather in the practical desire to control reality. Religion is not an obsolete version of pure science. It's a failed effort at applied sciences such as medicine or engineering.

Religion begins in magic, Frazer argues—for instance, in an effort to heal the sick or control the weather. But magic doesn't work, and so it evolves into religion: we try to meet such needs through prayers and exorcisms. When prayer fails, he explains, we can always say that the gods refused our prayers, and endeavor somehow to win the favor of the gods so they won't refuse the next time around. But over time, the repeated failure of prayer demonstrates the failure of religion. And according to Frazer, the failure of religion opens the door for science. Science succeeds where religion fails. Science allows us to control the world around us in pro-social ways.

The problem, of course, is that magic, science, and religion have coexisted for thousands of years. Magic is alive and well today, as countless websites attest. Many cultures globally have been both pervasively religious and quite ingenious in their engineering. In fact, it was a Christian theologian named John Philoponus who first insisted—contrary to Plato—that earthly reality had to be organized according to strictly rational laws, because the creator God is consummately rational.[1] But the prestige of Plato was so immense that the man's suggestion was ignored. That didn't change until Christian humanism in the 1300s began laying out in rigorous philosophical-theological terms an argument that the created world

---

1. Hart, *Atheist Delusions*, 69 and chapter 6 generally.

must have a rationally intelligible causal structure that reflects the perfect rationality of God.

Frazer make a second mistake as well, a far more subtle mistake. He confused the motives governing science itself with the motives governing how scientific discoveries are used by the surrounding culture. Science is a process of framing and testing hypotheses in an effort to develop a body of knowledge about predictable regularities in the natural world. It is a search for information and an effort to develop theories that hold an array of information in a configuration that elicits further fruitful research.

Whether or not the wider culture uses that information to serve the common good is another matter altogether. How scientific discoveries are *used* is a political and cultural issue, not a scientific issue. Science itself—as a method of inquiry—does not seek to control reality. The rest of us do.

Or we don't, as the case may be. If we lack the political will to use accurate information appropriately, research accumulates quietly in libraries and laboratories.

Just as religion is not trying to explain the predictable regularities of the physical world, science as a method of inquiry is not trying to save the world. Science is the human effort understand the world. Whether what scientists discover is put to "good use" or not depends upon everybody else.

Tylor, Frazer, and Evolution: Religion as "Primitive"

Tylor and Frazer arose within the same currents of European thought: they were both trying to apply evolutionary models to the study of religion. They did so through lenses provided by the philosopher Herbert Spenser, who was wildly popular at the time. But they made the same two mistakes. First, both of them agreed with Spenser (and behind Spenser, the botanist Charles Lyell) that evolution is a linear process leading directly from simple to complex forms: humans are more "highly evolved" than ferns or cockroaches. (Darwin did not make that mistake.)

Secondly, they transferred this mistake about biological evolution into a set of equally mistaken claims about cultural evolution.

Like Spenser himself, Tylor and Frazer assumed that different global cultures represent different stages in a natural evolution from naive or simple forms to sophisticated or complex forms. Just as children slowly mature into adults, so cultures gradually develop a "mature" array of concepts, attitudes, and beliefs.

Spenser's concept of "progress" combined with European cultural ethnocentricity to validate the belief that non-European cultures represent "childish" and "primitive" levels of intellectual development. For Tylor and Frazer, the antireligious late-Victorian European male mind represented the evolutionary and cultural apex of the human race. Everyone else, anyone else, could be dismissed as both "primitive" and "childish."

That belief justified both slavery and colonialism. It drove both the eugenics movement and what came to be called "Social Darwinism." Eventually it justified the Nazi death camps: Jews, Gypsies, LGBTQ individuals, the handicapped, and anyone who defied the regime were defectives to be eliminated as the naturally perfect Aryan male rose to dominate the globe. Stalinists took the same approach to anyone who questioned the Marxist ideology of the Soviet regime.

Spenserian social Darwinist "progress" also fueled the analysis of religion offered by Tylor and Frazer. Under "evolutionary" pressure from science, they argued, religion has become obsolete. Over time, they assumed, this vestigial religiosity would inevitably die out: people will realize that religion fails to deliver the control over material reality that only science can provide. Religion is doomed to extinction, all of its functions usurped. In the meantime, believers could be dismissed as "childish" or "primitive" thinkers—odd vestiges of our evolutionary past.

Behind the secularization thesis, behind the enormously influential analyses offered by Tylor and Frazer, stands a single key assumption: science and religion are in fact trying to do the same thing. Offhand, I can't decide whether that's a deeper misunderstanding of religious faith or of scientific inquiry.

4

The Secularization Thesis

The demise of religion predicted by Tylor and Frazer came to be called the "secularization thesis." It was orthodoxy among many social scientists throughout most of the 1900s—which testifies against the "scientific" authority of Tylor and Frazer, neither of whom were scientists. The secularization thesis also situated education itself as ideologically opposed to religion: smart people, educated people, will of course dismiss religion as nonsense.

As historian David Hollinger explains in *After Cloven Tongues of Fire* (2013), that trend was strongly reinforced by thinkers as widely influential as mid-Victorian biologist T. H. Huxley, philosopher John Dewey, and journalist Walter Lippman. All of them actively promoted dogmatic scientism as a religion—as the new religion that would save us from all the mistakes and all of the suffering human experience entails.

Dogmatic scientism in this new ideological sense would be a new and better infallible pope, a new and better inerrant Bible. This new dogmatic scientism would be the salvation of us all. It would once and for all solve the problems we face as a society.

Working scientists would be appalled by such claims. But grandiose descriptions of science as "the new religion of man" were remarkably influential in the first half of the twentieth century. Literal-minded Christians took at face value the self-aggrandizing of dogmatic scientism. And so they fought back. They saw the entire enterprise of legitimate science and social science as an effort to destroy Christianity. They demanded the right to protect their children from "indoctrination" in this rival faith.

The result was today's ongoing battles over biology textbooks and science curricula in public schools. That explains the ease with which the Religious Right can discredit whatever facts or scientific findings it becomes politically expedient to deny, whether denying climate research or stirring up religious opposition to universal health insurance.

Religious efforts to interfere in science education are scandalous nonsense. I've been clear on that point from the outset here. But there has also been scandalous nonsense from advocates of dogmatic scientism. For instance, Daniel Dennett, university professor and Director of the Center for Cognitive Studies at Tufts, claims that science has disproved the reality of the soul: "this idea of immaterial souls, capable of defying the laws of physics, has outlived its credibility thanks to the advance of the natural sciences."[1] But "soul" is a theological concept. The natural sciences investigate the natural world; they do not and never have investigated "the immaterial soul" nor any other theological concept. Dennet fails to understand what theologians and believers mean by "the soul" just as literal-minded believers fail to understand "evolution" as a concept.

Another example: Richard Dawkins is an evolutionary biologist who served for thirteen years as the Simonyi Professor for the Public Understanding of Science at Oxford University. He has argued that religion is a cultural virus that ought to be exterminated. His claims of "scientific" legitimacy for such an attitude have been soundly refuted. Both Dennet and Dawkins have been sharply criticized by serious book reviewers and again at length by thinkers like John Dupré, Terry Eagleton, and Mary Midgley. There is no need for me to rehearse the issue. My point here is much simpler: given the prominence of Dawkins's position, or Dennett's, such claims have been quite nearly catastrophic for the public understanding of science.

1. Dennett, *Freedom Evolves*, 1.

I don't say this in some a rear-guard effort to defend religious assaults on science education. My point is a historical one: the clash of absolutisms that arose among the Victorians continues today. And that's a problem for all of us.

The Secularization Thesis Reconsidered

One of the major arguments in support of the secularization thesis is the fact that religious participation has been declining steeply. Christianity is quite nearly extinct in Europe. For a long time religion was robustly present in the US, as it is in the rest of the globe; but now the Millennial generation is turning out to be increasingly secular. Is that proof that the secularization thesis is correct after all? Is Christianity culturally "primitive" or perhaps a mode of thought radically incompatible with empirical science?

No, in a word. But that's an important question, so let's stop here for a minute to think about it. Charles Taylor's *A Secular Age* (2007) offers a far more nuanced account of the rise of secularity than anything Tylor or Frazer ever imagined. Taylor attributes the rise of European secularism not to the rise of science but to cultural revulsion at theological developments within Christianity itself. His argument in support of that claim tops out at nearly a thousand pages: he offers broad, rigorous primary evidence supported by arguments that are both historically and psychologically nuanced. *A Secular Age* is both massive and massively convincing.

Secularism arose, he explains, because Protestant theologians made a set of closely related mistakes. These mistakes echoed and re-echoed throughout Europe, which remained firmly committed to the political unity of church and state.

First, and in the 1500s, Calvinist accounts of God's absolute omnipotence were elaborated into the doctrine of predestination. According to the doctrine of predestination, the vast majority of humanity will go to hell no matter what. Our behavior does not matter: our fate has been sealed from all eternity. We will go to hell because even the most virtuous among us fails to meet God's moral standards. All of humanity is "innately depraved." God has chosen to save a few people from eternal torment in hell, but not because they deserve salvation and the rest of us don't. None of us deserve anything other than eternal suffering in hell.

But if we are all innately depraved, then no one should trust individual conscience. Authority is crucial. Democracy is theologically suspect. In short, Calvin and Luther were not the proponents of individual freedom they are sometimes made out to be. Yes, they insisted that individuals should be able to read the Bible for themselves. But in their systems of thought, "The Bible" exerts absolute control over the population. They never dreamed that church and state could be or should be separated. Western Christian theocracy should continue unabated, but now in a revised, less decadent, less abusive form than the imperial papacy of the Middle Ages.

Second, given the fact that all of humanity is innately depraved, Protestants eagerly enlisted state authority to enforce private morality. That's why, even today, some jurisdictions flatly forbid the sale of alcohol or why, for so many decades, businesses were forced to close on Sunday. Even in Chicago, one could not buy a bottle of wine in a grocery store on Sunday morning: a postcard announcing a change in that policy arrived in the mail just yesterday.

This effort to enlist state authority echoes even today in religious efforts to bar access to insurance coverage for birth control or to ban abortion even in cases of rape, incest, hazard to the mother's life, a nonviable fetus, and so forth. Such strategies are unabashedly theocratic: imagine American Hindus or Buddhists trying to ban the sale of meat in the US because their religions demands vegetarianism. That's what authoritarian theocrats in the Christian tradition are trying to do. The issue here is not whether abortion is immoral in some circumstances: there are important religious arguments to be made on that topic. The issue at stake is whether a minority group—one particular subset of one particular religion—can be allowed to impede the legal rights of other Americans.

Needless to say, Taylor argues, reasonable people in the 1500s and 1600s were quite unhappy when radical Protestants set about enforcing rigorous moral norms upon entire populations, even while insisting that most of people are damned to hell even if they obey.

In a third strategy, radical Protestants put an end to religious art such as sculpture, painting, and stained-glass windows. An enormous artistic heritage was smashed, often by mobs, in the kind of rampages that the twentieth century witnessed in China's devastating Cultural Revolution or, more recently, in Taliban attacks on Buddhist sculpture in Afghanistan, Sunni attacks on Shia religious architecture, and so forth.

With the loss of this art came the loss of both the private and the communal spirituality that had centered around these artistic traditions. Much of Europe's heritage of religious music was silenced in favor of extremely simple congregational singing of psalms. Even that much was deeply controversial. What lay behind this radical antagonism to art was a narrow redefinition of faith as intellectual assent to creeds and other doctrinal claims—which is to say, of course, deference to the authority of institutional leaders who controlled the content and interpretation of such doctrines.

In effect, Taylor explains, Protestant Christianity lopped off most of what had made Christianity deeply relevant to ordinary life. As a religion, Christianity lost most of its own spirituality. With their relentless focus on escaping the wrath of God and "getting to heaven," radical Protestant sects neglected the more immediately spiritual task of sustaining supportive community, encouraging resilience, and consoling our suffering. Christianity stopped making humanly relevant sense of the immediate experience of daily life. Planting and harvesting, for instance, were no longer universally celebrated with an ancient mix of religious ritual and communal merriment.

Christine Leigh Heyrman situates this process in a uniquely American context in her very readable history, *Southern Cross: The Beginnings of the Bible Belt* (1997). The Great Awakenings tried to stop the parties surrounding barn raising, quilting bees, and other happy occasions sustaining social networks.

I stumbled into this reality one day when my writing group moved to a Presbyterian church parlor. (Our expected hostess cancelled at the last moment, pleading a plumbing emergency.) It was my turn to bring beer, so I walked in with a cold six-pack: one beer for each of us. One. All of us over fifty.

The world nearly ended. And then it nearly ended a second time when I laughed at their dismay. But then I got up to return the booze to my car: enough of this, I thought. Courtesy is courtesy: it's their church.

But as I got up, forgiveness began to flow: I was Irish, somebody said. Worse yet, someone pointed out, I was Catholic born and bred. If anyone saw us drinking beer, I could be blamed: clueless Cate, sweet clueless Cate, one of those decadent Irish Catholics who don't understand the first thing about Christianity.

The beers were opened and passed around. Nonetheless, the parlor door was kept closed, the beers drunk quickly and furtively. I was flabbergasted—until I read *Southern Cross*.

As both Heyrman and Taylor argue, the goal of faith became pie in the sky when you die, not a meaningful life here and now. But pie in the sky when you die, if it happens, is God's own arbitrary choice. Your fate was sealed from time immemorial. As Heyrman documents in painful detail, that claim caused untold anguish for many. It still does. I have heard a lot of that from good folks over the years.

Worse yet, Taylor explains, was a fourth line of thinking. It goes like this. If God is both radically distant and relentlessly vindictive against massively corrupt humanity—you included—then the churches have nothing to offer that is remotely as comforting as deciding that God is an illusion and Christianity is superstitious nonsense. Why bother with belief? Slowly but surely, Taylor explains, people began to disengage and then to walk away.

And that, he contends, explains the rise of secularism, especially in the historically Protestant European nations. In short: secularism arose in reaction against theological changes within Christianity itself, not in response to the rise of science. If Christianity is culturally doomed, it is doomed from within. Science has nothing to do with it—real science, that is, the ordinary work done in ordinary labs.

But the truly radical theological positions taken by a few leaders in succeeding generations of Protestant reformers could not and did not eradicate the spiritual and religious wisdom that Christianity had acquired over the preceding 1,500 years. Personal spirituality set about reviving itself. These days even Protestants do meditation practice. They walk labyrinths. They engage in ancient religious rituals. They repeat very ancient patterns of daily prayer. Religious chant has staged a major comeback. Those who did remain Christian amidst the rise of secularism and religious radicalism either sustained or rapidly recreated systems of social support and personal meaning.

In *Faith No More: Why People Reject Religion* (2012), Phil Zuckerman interviews a wide array of individuals who have left absolutist, biblically literalist, rigidly judgmental churches. Across the board, they lament the loss of warm, closely knit, supportive community and the sense of personal meaning that their faith once provided. They leave because they have quite intelligent questions that no one is capable of answering to their satisfaction. For them, the intellectual piece is missing—and they find themselves unwilling to do without it.

What they are rejecting, then, is a particular version of Christianity. What they fail to recognize—what Zuckerman himself fails to recognize—is that there are altogether different versions of Christianity out there. There are traditions within Christianity where their honest questions might find honest and honestly satisfying answers.

5

God the Engineer Almighty

Here's a curious fact about Tylor and Frazer: given the flaws in their
evidence, their ideas still have remarkable currency as something
like the "folklore" of the religion-versus-science debate. That in-
trigues me. Why is that the case? How could that be the case?

Their analyses still have cultural credibility, I suggest, because
many people (including some believers) implicitly share their core
assumptions about who God is supposed to be—and thus what
religious faith is supposed to entail. And why? Because Tylor and
Frazer were reflecting the folklore-level theology of mid-Victorian
England. That folklore-level theology has a marvelous back story

As Victorians, Sir Edward Tylor and Sir James Frazer inherited an Enlightenment-era cosmology: the universe was pictured
as a single, vast, slowly ticking mechanical device. It was ruled by
causal principles as simple and logical as Euclidean geometry and
classic Newtonian physics. In this naively "Newtonian" or mecha-
nist world view, there is a scientific law explaining every possible
event. We may not know that law yet, of course. But by definition,
there is a scientific law accounting for everything.

As I explain in more detail in *Confronting Religious Absolutism* [forthcoming], chapter 5, the development of this cosmology
constituted a crisis for Christianity. In a naively "Newtonian" or
mechanistic cosmos, a potential event is either law governed or it is

impossible. There is no middle ground. And any event that violates an established scientific law is by definition either an illusion or a lie. Nothing happens that science cannot explain—even if we can't explain it yet.

Given that mechanistic world view, some would argue that it's a waste of time to pray that God will disrupt causality to solve some problem for us: these laws cannot be broken. Miracles are "scientifically impossible" in a mechanistic, rule-governed cosmos. Some Christians would reply, of course, that laws which God has written God is also free to suspend or disrupt if God so desires. This line of argument turns "miracles" into crucial evidence for the existence of God. The dispute over miracles becomes part of the cultural crisis triggering the rise of Victorian absolutism in the Christian tradition: one way or another, whether through an inerrant Bible or an infallible pope, Christian fundamentalism insists that God is in charge of absolutely everything, not the so-called scientific "laws" of a naively "Newtonian" or mechanistic cosmology. And proof of God's absolute power, or so the argument goes, is God's ability to overrule the causal regularities of the material world.

In this chapter, I want to critique this theological claim about God and causality. Then I'll make a series of closely related points. First: the rise of what I will call "Engineer Almighty" theology demonstrates that theology is in significant ways culturally constructed. For better for worse, it reflects the world view of its own day. Second, and as a result: what we believe at any given point about God therefore says a lot about *us*. This entire line of analysis comes down to what anthropologist Clifford Geertz famously argued in 1966: a religion is a system of symbols that motivates and explains human behavior. In thinking about Geertz's insight over a period of weeks, I realized something that stopped me cold: both Christian fundamentalism and the cultural efforts to transform empirical science into dogmatic scientism are part of the same trend in Western culture. They both reflect the late Victorian drive toward totalitarian ideologies generally.

In short: there's a lot at stake here. More on that at the end of this chapter. First we need to take a good hard look at the Engineer Almighty.

The Birth of the Engineer Almighty

Beginning with the publication of Newton's remarkable work, and under the influence of a highly mechanized world view crudely derived from his work, the West began to picture God as something like the Engineer Almighty.

The Engineer Almighty is responsible for designing and managing all the day-to-day operations of this vast and rationally quantifiable cosmic mechanism. Everything that happens—absolutely everything—somehow reflects "the will of God," because God in effect wrote and continues to manage the source code running the cosmos. Events around us are "God's will" by definition. God is, in effect, the personification of naively "Newtonian" scientific causality according to which every possible event is rationally rule-governed even if we cannot yet describe that rule in scientific terms. Newtonian Causality Personified is a role God inherited along with his earlier heritage as the Platonic "*nous*," or mind, whose ideas are the prototypes behind the models whose shadows we mistakenly call "the real world."

Redefining God as the Engineer Almighty was all the more inevitable given the theological influence of John Calvin. Calvin's theology included an absolutist account of God's "omnipotence." This tendency in Calvin was exaggerated by subsequent generations of far more radical church leaders and, of course, popular culture as a whole. Over time, God was redefined as something worse than the personification of scientific causality. Over time, God was redefined as the dark projection of our own most neurotic control needs, with all the potential for violence that such anxieties entail. As documented at length in the book and documentary film *With God on Our Side: The Rise of the Religious Right* (1996), televangelists have traditionally preyed upon such anxieties, coordinating with radical right-wing political organizers to reap votes.

The more literally you buy into this Engineer Almighty theology, the more clearly prayer will look like a call to tech support. Or more simply yet, prayer becomes something like dropping quarters into God the Cosmic Vending Machine—a vending machine that swallows our quarters without yielding up the goodies we seek.

These theological models of God are plainly liable to the critiques offered by Tylor and by Frazer.

Theological Problems with the Engineer Almighty

We are not Victorians. Our world view has changed. Heirs of quantum physics and chaos theory, we no longer see the world as a vast, simply rational "Newtonian" mechanism. As a result, the "scientific" foundation of God the Engineer Almighty theology is now an outmoded science. That fact renders the God the Engineer Almighty doubly irrelevant: he doesn't deliver, and the foundation on which he should have been able to deliver does not in fact exist. This is a God with a serious problem.

When literal-minded Christian absolutists insist that global climate change is theologically impossible, or that Genesis trumps evolution, or that the age of the earth is to be determined by counting biblical generations, not by the findings of geologists and astrophysicists, then bystanders have reason to conclude that Christianity is something like a cultural zombie. My faith looks like an undead thought system threatening to wreak havoc on the rest of us by interfering with scientifically solid problem solving. I understand that perception.

And I reply that the Engineer Almighty is just as incoherent theologically as he is scientifically. I can't say that strongly enough. The theological problem is not that science has long since discarded simple Newtonian mechanics as a model of reality. The theological problem is this: God the Engineer Almighty, did he exist, would be demonic.

Such a God, did he exist, would be morally responsible for causing—or for failing to prevent—the sum total of human suffering. At a bare minimum, God the Engineer Almighty would rightly be charged with criminal negligence for designing a system where horrific human suffering is both widespread and inescapable. The usual defense is that God has granted us free will, a gift that we have abused. But horrific diseases, disabilities, and natural disasters are not the result of human free will: far too much agony is left unaccounted for by the usual "free will" defense. Furthermore, the free will defense might work if it were not widely assumed that God is capable of creating a more perfect reality whether in heaven or here on earth after the putative second coming. What happens to free will in this more perfect reality? If God is capable of such an extraordinary system update, then God is morally accountable for failing to release that update long before now.

Beyond that Engineer: A Changing View of God

I'll get back to these difficult theological questions in *The Confrontational Wit of Jesus* [forthcoming], chapter 11. For now, let's stay with cultural history. God the Engineer Almighty may appear to be the only possible God. That is not the case. God the Engineer Almighty is a God whose cultural viability ended with the "death of God" movement that peaked in the mid-twentieth century. The God who "died" at that point was this blessed engineer. Lots of people panicked at the thought. To paraphrase Nietzsche, if the Engineer Almighty is dead, then all things are permitted, because the cosmic role of that God was keeping order by threatening the endless torture of sinners.

Let me begin here with an obvious point: Christian theology changes. It has changed quite dramatically in the past, and it is changing again today in quite remarkable ways. The tradition has thought about God in many ways, even though at any one point the tradition appears to claim that this is how people have always thought.

And here's another small, plain, historical-cultural fact: how we imagine God says a lot about us. If we define God as "overwhelming, indomitable power," then we are all too likely to seek such power for ourselves, and to organize our social structures along authoritarian lines. We will do so because "what God demands of us" is also a cultural code for "what we can demand of one another." For instance, if God demands complete sexual abstinence except for the purpose of getting pregnant, then it might seem legitimate for me to outlaw birth control—or at least make it both difficult to acquire and prohibitively expensive.

More dangerously yet, how God enforces God's demands is also a cultural code for how we can enforce our own demands. God punishes sinners and non-Christians alike with horrific torture for an eternity? Such a violent God implicitly demonstrates that violence against others can be morally justified. As a result, inflicting horrific pain can be a morally appropriate human behavior too. As many have noted, literal-minded Christians on the far Right broadly support capital punishment, torture, concealed-carry gun laws, and preemptive military attacks on other nations.

I focus directly on the question of whether Christianity is inherently violent in *Confronting Religious Violence*, chapter 9, and whether Christianity is sexually obsessed bigotry in *Confronting Religious Denial of Gay Marriage*, chapter 5. For now I'd like to point out that there's a flip side to what our theology reveals about us and our own values. It is equally the case that how we imagine the world around us has a massive impact on how we think about God.

Every world view has its equivalent theology. By the same measure, every trend in philosophy has its equivalent movement in theology. The study of such dynamics, century by century by century, is called "historical theology." Even a little historical theology can go a very long way toward convincing anyone that our ideas about God are socially and culturally constructed.

Clifford Geertz: Religion as a System of Symbols

In some ways, what I'm saying here is what anthropologist Clifford Geertz said in a widely influential essay in 1966. Geertz defines culture itself as "an historically transmitted pattern of meanings embodied in symbols." Religion is one of these systems of symbols, he explains.

Specifically, religion is a system of symbols connecting our world view with our behavior. Here is exactly what he says—a very famous definition:

> Religion is (1) a system of symbols which act to (2) establish powerful, pervasive, and long-lasting moods and motivations in men by (3) formulating conceptions of a general order of existence and (4) clothing these

conceptions with such an aura of factuality that (5) the
moods and motivations seem uniquely realistic.[1]

It seems to me that Geertz's definition explains what anyone ought
to be able to see from the careful study of historical theology: an
era's ideas about God both influence and are influenced by everything else going on at the time.

That's why imagination as a cognitive ability is essential both
to religion and to the study of religion: imagination is our ability
both to forge symbolism and to grapple intelligently with the many
different systems of symbols that organize our culture at any particular moment. Within a culture, religion may be uniquely powerful in its ability to forge a dynamic connection between individual
behavior and the cultural symbolic matrices in play in a given era.

Some believers might object sharply to defining Christianity
as a system of symbols. They might object because that seems to
reduce Christianity to something arbitrary, superficial, and altogether disposable. Geertz's definition might strike some people as
altogether reductive—and hence deeply objectionable.

That is not the case. It would be the case, however, if by "symbol" one means nothing more than "sign." I discuss the difference
in detail in *Confronting Religious Absolutism* [forthcoming], chapters 11 and 12. At this point all we need is a quick sketch of the
essentials. A sign is extrinsic to what it signifies: there's nothing
inherent in a red octagon that a red octagon signals "stop." A blue
circle would work just as successfully if that's what we were used to
seeing. A symbol, on the other hand, is deeply intrinsic to what it
signifies. And symbolism, thus properly understood, is one of our
most sophisticated and subtle cognitive abilities for grappling with
the paradoxes that inform a complicated, messy reality.

To dismiss religion across the board because it is "merely"
a system of symbols is like dismissing particle physics across the
board because it's perfectly obvious that material reality is made up
of solid *things*, not the teensy irrationally leaping specks of energy
that particle physicists carry on about. A believer who thinks I am
guilty of dismissing or denigrating the faith that we share has failed

1. Geertz, "Religion as a Cultural System," 3.

to understand just how serious and how substantial symbolism actually is. Symbolism is the cognitive strategy whereby we both grasp and share the most sophisticated truths we are capable of grasping. To shrug dismissively and say "just a symbol" is like shrugging dismissively and saying, "just a speck of energy."

Totalitarianism and the Rise of Fundamentalism

As I struggled with these issues, slowly assembling the analysis I've dubbed "the Engineer Almighty," I realized something. It unnerved me acutely. It dawned on me quite suddenly as I stood in line one day at my local Panera, waiting to order a salad for lunch. Here's the problem: there's a clear relationship between totalitarian ideologies and God as imagined by religious fundamentalists. That's dangerous. This link between totalitarianism and fundamentalism may explain the rise of fundamentalist religion as a global source of violent conflict.

Jonathan Sacks had already made that point, I realized later, in his lyrical *The Dignity of Difference: How to Avoid the Clash of Civilizations* (2002). What's clashing in the rise of religiously motivated violence is competing totalitarian ideologies, not civilizations. But when a religion moves toward fundamentalist totalitarianism, it drags its civilization along—destroying ancient moral and spiritual resources in the process.

The theological issues involved here are many and complex; I don't want to detour into those abstruse theological arguments. But even at the most superficial level, the perfection of God was not traditionally imagined as a perfection of absolutist causal control. The perfection of God in Hebrew Scriptures is a quality called "*chesed*," usually translated "loving-kindness." In the late second century BCE, when the Jews translated their Scriptures from Hebrew into Greek, "*chesed*" was translated into the Greek word "*agape*." And "*agape*," in turn, is usually translated into English as "love." Christian Scriptures were written in Greek, not Hebrew: when these writers assert that God is love, the word they use is "*agape*." Whether in English we say "love" or "loving-kindness" or "compassion," we are describing the same quality.

As Martin Luther insisted, God loves all of humanity because of who God is, and not because of anything we have done or refrained from doing. Love is God's very nature. Compassion is God's very nature. Causal control or "scientific law" is something else again.

The God of infinite compassion and radically inclusive loving-kindness is not a vending machine. Such a God is neither a casual principle nor "Newtonian" mechanism personified. Nonetheless, "Engineer Almighty" theology has persisted as a tremendously powerful idea in Western culture. In religious terms, it generates the God of fundamentalism.

In secular terms, it generates absolutist or totalitarian ideologies. Let me explain how that happens. When Nietzsche proclaimed "the death of God" in 1882, the divinity in question was the Engineer Almighty. But soon enough this character reappeared in secular form and modern dress, because of course the Newtonian world view still held sway. Across the turn from the nineteenth to the twentieth century, thinkers in many fields proposed that there exists something, some one thing, which calls all the shots. Its power is absolute. It cannot be escaped. Its legitimacy cannot be questioned. Its existence explains everything. But it is hidden from direct view. It can only be known indirectly, by excavation and by inference undertaken by "priestly" experts, whose ranks only the select can attain. Nonetheless, it controls our behavior. Its control over our society is absolute—and absolutely beyond question.

Nominees for this new absolute appeared all across the intellectual landscape. For many thinkers, the Freudian unconscious or the Jungian collective unconscious explained everything. For Stalin and others, it was Marx's dialectical materialism. Still others explained everything by reference to Adam's Smith's "invisible hand" of the free market. For Hitler, it was Herbert Spenser's theory of evolution. What all these developments have in common is this: by definition, fundamentalist ideology cannot imagine that it might be mistaken. Its orthodoxy is rigid and absolute. It is immune from demands for evidence and consistent logic. It is immune from doubt: believe and be saved; doubt and be damned.

In the midst of this secularized "theological" development, of course dogmatic scientism came to function for some people in exactly the same way. It provides absolute truth. It ought to take control of all other varieties of inquiry and sources of truth in the culture. Dogmatic scientism and fundamentalist Christianity are then in a zero-sum contest for the allegiance of the population because totalitarian systems brook no rivals. That's what defines "totalitarianism" in the first place.

Such hyperbolic, totalitarian claims about dogmatic scientism outrage many working scientists, just as the fulminations of the Religious Right leave many Christians fuming. But as a Christian, my responsibility here is to Christian fundamentalism. My concern here is simple and pointed: Christian fundamentalism must not triumph in its effort to get control of what "Christianity" means culturally—as a "brand," to speak crudely. When otherwise-sophisticated thinkers dismiss Christians out of hand and across the board, they are in effect ceding cultural control to the radical Religious Right. Such casual, contemptuous dismissal of Christianity by the learned—and I've heard it repeatedly over the years—in effect concedes the "brand" to fundamentalists.

You don't have to share my faith—not for a moment—to realize how dangerous that would be. Ceding Christianity across the board to the worst representative of Christianity is like thinking that science across the board is accurately represented by the Tuskegee experiments on African American men. The Christian cultural heritage has enormous persuasive power in Western culture. Whether we realize it or not, whether we are believers or not, Christianity is something like the source code—the repository of images and stories—whereby the West thinks about human identity and moral responsibility.

This source code must not fall into the wrong hands. Or to the extent that this has already happened, even the most skeptical of nonbelievers need to know enough cultural history to distinguish between hard-Right Christian radicals and the mainstream religious tradition.

Christianity, Cultural Change, and Problem Solving

If "Christianity" comes to be defined by fundamentalists, then we will lose a cultural tradition of vital practical importance. We will lose a powerful set of specifically Western cultural resources for solving what are now global technical problems like climate change, regulating a global economy, and remedying unsustainable trends in economic disparity. Science cannot solve problems like these. Economic quants can't solve problems like these. To solve these problems, we need something much more subtle than massively complex technical analyses of the problem itself.

Facts and analyses of facts are necessary, of course. But they are not sufficient. If solid technical analysis of global climate change data were enough, we would already have addressed that problem. But facts alone are never enough to elicit broad cultural change, especially not on a global scale. Neither is the absolutist authority claimed by the fundamentalists. The twentieth century tried totalitarianism. It doesn't work. It was as catastrophic a development as the crusades or the great wars of religion in 1524–1660.

But we need broad cultural change if we expect to avert the catastrophes looming on a short horizon—clearly within the next 500 years, and probably much sooner. And religion—ancient, subtle, spiritually astute religion—has the resources to effect significant cultural change. It's the only cultural resource we have for non-coercive personal change—change in what Geertz called our "moods and motivations" and in the "general order of existence" that is our world view. The way we are living now is not sustainable, but we do not lack the cultural resources for the changes we need.

The problem is that fundamentalist Christians have so discredited and disgraced what Jesus taught that increasing numbers of Americans want nothing whatever to do with Christians. That matters, because Christianity as a symbolic system in Geertz's sense has something like highly developed antibodies to such classic Western dysfunctions as excessive individualism, consumerism, ideological defense of economic exploitation, and neglect of both the common good and the environment.

I'm not saying that only the West has these problems. The Chinese, for instance, are notorious for poisoning the environment; the Indians pursue individual economic gain while ignoring malnutrition in a majority of their nation's children. But in the West, equivalent moral failings take a distinctively Western character, and Christianity has equally distinctive remedies.

These remedies exist within the traditional spiritual practices that Western Christianity mostly jettisoned under combined pressure from the Protestant Reformation and the European Enlightenment, which had a massive influence on Protestants and Catholics alike. But before I can explain something about these resources—prayer, for instance—I need to say a little more about Geertz's concept that religion is a system of symbols.

Christianity is not that unchanging set of propositional claims known as "dogmas" and "doctrines."

6

Christianity as a System of Symbols

In this chapter I want to explore how Christianity functions not as a rival for science but as a symbolic diagnosis of the human condition: what's wrong; why we suffer; what we can do about any of that. This symbolic diagnosis is the core of Christian spirituality. But I do not intend to begin in the usual place, which would be some summary account of theologically adequate teachings about God or Jesus. I want to start with evolutionary psychology—and then work my way to pondering an obvious fact: if religion is a system of symbols, we have to consider seriously that "symbolism" is an explicitly literary strategy of meaning. Nothing is symbolic all by itself. An element in a narrative becomes symbolic through the role it comes to play in the narrative as the plot unfolds.

More on the later, of course. First we need to look at what social science has to say about how these systems of symbols arise in human culture.

In *Darwin's Cathedral: Evolution, Religion, and the Nature of Society* (2002), evolutionary biologist David Sloan Wilson argues that religion is an evolved disposition to create symbolic structures that motivate pro-social behaviors. That's why it's ubiquitous in human cultures. Religions can contribute significantly to the central evolutionary task of surviving and reproducing. Religions can help us to maintain healthy, high-functioning groups that provide categories of benefit available to us only through cooperation with others.

Frans de Waal argues a closely related point in his work on animal ethnology, work nicely summarized in *Primates and Philosophers: How Morality Evolves* (2006). He contends that pro-social behavior depends upon neurological complexity, principally the physical ability to see and understand another's point of view. That capacity makes complex social organization possible, and so it exists among other social animals. In them we see the beginnings of collaborative problem solving and non-self-centered compassion. The capacity for such complex behavior is dependent upon neurological complexity. Among social animals, de Waal argues, such complexity is selected for. What animals can't do that people are only beginning to learn, de Waal concludes somewhat sadly, is to overcome the absolute boundary between Us and Them. Among social animals, compassion and collaboration are sharply limited to the Us group. People might do better than that. And if we can't, then given our extraordinary intellectual abilities, out-group animosity may be the end of all of us.

Religions do not always function in the pro-social way that Wilson describes. Or if religious do function pro-socially, it may be be only for the benefit of the in-group, the Us-group. We all know that. Religions can turn toxic, or developments within a religion can become toxic. Human cognitive skills can always be turned to toxic ends. But religion is nearly universal in human cultures, Wilson argues, because we have an innate disposition to create symbolic structures that help us get along.

I'm intrigued by such arguments, and I'm impressed by Wilson's simultaneous academic appointments in biology and in anthropology. If human morality is literally something that Moses carried down from the mountain carved by God in stone, then all of us are doomed. Morality cannot come from outside the human character. Morality cannot be successfully imposed upon us by external authority. Morality must be deeply rooted in the biological facts of our cognitive capacities and our innate sociability. If it isn't, our capacity for greed and for violence will eventually destroy us all.

His Holiness the Dalai Lama has written two recent and very thought-provoking books substantiating Wilson's claims from within the theological and scriptural resources of major global religions. In *Toward a True Kinship of Faiths: How the World's Religions Can Come Together* (2010), he lays out the different conceptual bases on which different religions advocate pro-social behaviors such as compassion, integrity, control of appetites, a modest lifestyle, and responsibility for the common good. These conceptual foundations differ, but there is remarkable agreement about what Geertz would call the "motives and behaviors" that each solicits from believers. In *Beyond Religion: Ethics for the Whole World* (2011), the Dalai Lama extends his analysis to include secular humanism. He argues that there are also purely secular arguments to be made for compassion, commitment to the common good, and so forth. Greg Epstein makes a similar argument in *Good without God* (2009).

Extensive empirical support for such claims has been laid out by Richard Wilkinson and Kate Pickett, a pair of British epidemiologists, in *The Spirit Level: Why Greater Equality Makes Societies Stronger* (2009). In their book, graph after graph after graph demonstrates that, even for the very wealthiest segment of a society, outcomes are worse in countries with greater disparities in wealth and human well-being. For instance, life expectancies for the very wealthiest Americans or Brits are nonetheless lower than life expectancies for the top tier in countries that are far more economically egalitarian—even though the wealthiest in egalitarian societies have lower personal incomes. That's only one of the dozens of data sets that they analyze.

In short, arguing for compassion is not difficult. Nor is it difficult to understand or to explain the core differences between right and wrong. There are many different conceptual bases from which to do that successfully. Theory is not the problem. The problem is practice. What successfully moves the "motivations and behaviors" of a population toward compassion and responsibility for the common good? That's the problem. We have trouble getting from theory to practice.

Theory, Practice, and Truth

The relationship between theory and practice matters acutely. Wilson gestures toward this relationship when he notes, almost in passing, that "the effectiveness of some symbolic systems evidently requires believing that they are factually correct."[1]

It's not at all clear what he means by "factually correct." In a Christian context, that might mean biblical literalism. Creation happened in six days, the Red Sea parted when Moses held up his hand, Jesus walked on the water and furthermore walked out of his tomb after being miraculously resuscitated. "Factually correct" might mean that the fundamentalists are right after all: for Christianity to be an effective source of pro-social behavior, believers have to take these ancient narratives as something like high-level journalism, telling us "what really happened" with divinely guaranteed literal-factual accuracy. That's what fundamentalists insist, after all: there is a the slippery slope from doubting that Scripture is God's very words to the abyss of moral chaos.

So what does Wilson mean by "factually correct"? The question matters because I agree with the Dalai Lama: we can neither discard nor attempt to reconcile the disparate symbolic systems and conceptual foundations upon which various religions advocate for the common good. To be effective, Christianity has to be grounded in solid, intellectually respectable truth claims. The problem, then, is truth about what? Truth about creation happening in six days six thousand years ago? Or truth about something else?

Symbolism and Story

Like other religions, each in its own way, Christianity offers truth about the human condition. It offers spiritual wisdom and insight, not biology and geology. Christianity explores the complexity of the human spirit and the intricacies of human experience. It anchors its understanding of that complexity in claims about the ultimate reality "behind" reality as humanly known: the reality of God. Great

1. Wilson, *Darwin's Cathedral*, 229

preachers and liturgists offer such wisdom week after week after week.

There may not be enough great preachers and liturgists. But there are not enough artists of high enough caliber in any field you might want to imagine. And simultaneously there are far more of them than outsiders realize. Similarly, you might be amazed by the local musicians playing at the coffeehouse on the corner on any given Saturday night. Or the art being produced at your community arts studio, or the quality of the productions at your community theater. Or the performances of your community symphony orchestra. Is it world class? Maybe not. Can it take your breath away regardless? You bet it can.

As I have already explained, Christian insight into the human condition is expressed through what social scientists like Geertz and Wilson label "systems of symbols." But here I want to make a rudimentary observation: symbolism is a literary strategy of meaning. Nothing is "symbolic" all by itself. Something becomes symbolic through the role it plays in the stories we tell.

Christianity, like other religions, has an immense array of compelling and vivid stories. These stories are elaborate and engaging, dramatic and diverse, retold and refined and reinterpreted over thousands of years. What's "factually correct" about Christianity is not creation in six days, nor Jesus walking on the water. What's factually true about Christianity is its core vision of the human condition, which is the ultimate truth conveyed by the symbolic system generated by this immense heritage of stories told and retold.

At the risk of radical simplification, I contend that the core Christian vision comes down to this: we make one another miserable. Hell is other people, as Sartre said. Or as the ancients said, *homo homini lupus*. Man is wolf to man. The pain and suffering inherent in our biological mortality is bad enough, but it does not hold a candle to the pain and suffering imposed by human greed, violence, and self-centered indifference. The world would not become a perfect place if we stopped abusing one another. But the sum total of human grief would be remarkably reduced.

The human predicament is that we find ourselves trapped within political, social, and economic systems that exploit the many for the gain of the few. Historians and historical economists argue that this has been the case from the rise of the very first civilization anywhere on the globe. Within these systems, the rest of us scramble to do the best we can for ourselves and our families. If we look up at all from this state of affairs, it is only to be grateful that we are not trapped in some slave factory in China, or imprisoned in the sex trade in Thailand, or starving to death in a refugee camp. But mostly we don't look up at all. We are scrambling too hard just to survive: this wider view is unbearable to consider.

As Geertz might warn, these oppressive arrangements are embodied by interlocking systems of cultural symbols that appear to be "uniquely realistic." We are trapped in a rat race that feels for all the world inescapable, objective, and necessary. Unregulated global finance and crony capitalism is a religion of sorts too, and its essential doctrines are familiar to any of us. Nice guys finish last. Get the most; give the least. He who dies with the most toys wins. Look out for #1. The bottom line is the top priority. And the result? Thoreau said it best: "The mass of men lead lives of quiet desperation."[2] That was in 1854.

Christianity argues that the suffering we impose upon one another is neither inescapable nor necessary. There is an alternative. It is both costly and dangerous, as the death of Jesus illustrated. Seen in that light, there's something more than pious sentimentality in the ancient Jewish commandment to welcome the immigrant and to love our neighbors as ourselves. Such demands have a sharp socioeconomic edge. They call us to confront the massively antisocial cultural systems that surround us.

And Yet . . .

But what does that mean? For years, that was my question. At street level, what does that ancient Jewish-Christian claim mean in my life? How exactly am I suppose to do this? Tell me: how does this play out amidst the nitty-gritty of my own calendar with its sidebar list of things to do? How does it play out amidst the messiness of

2. Thoreau, *Walden and Civil Disobedience*, 5.

my relationships with friends and family and colleagues and all the competing priorities these relationships entail? How?

The Christian answer to my question *but how?* is not simple-minded authoritarian advice, nor rigidly petty moralism, nor a legislative agenda. Christianity is not a political party with stained-glass windows. Jesus was not a policy wonk. The answer to my angry, frustrated question, I have discovered, is not a detailed list of things to do or policies to support.

It's a story. Story after story. Stories alluding to and arguing with other stories. Commentaries on stories. Critical studies of the historical context and allusions and literary conventions of stories. And, of course, the ongoing invitation to locate my own story amidst these stories, to see for myself, in the symbolic resonance of all these stories, the wisdom and the help I need in navigating the story that is my own life. Stories offer invitations, not easy answers.

If we take these stories literally, merely as accounts of events, then all we get are events from thousands of years ago—some of them fairly dubious. The meaning of this old event for our own lives remains to be determined by something else outside of the event itself, typically some doctrine or dogma. But if we take the stories as stories—as vehicles for symbolic meanings or symbolic insights that can be conveyed in no other way—then our focus will be on those symbolic meanings. Our focus will be on locating our own stories by analogy to the inherited story.

What the scriptural story means for my story is for me to figure out. For you, it is for you to determine. That is both less precise and symbolically far more durable than any policy proposal ever could be. These stories have been read and reread, interpreted and reinterpreted, for thousands of years. Many of them have the extraordinarily symbolic density found in classic mythological sources, folk tales, and so forth.

Stories embody and convey meanings with a subtlety and complexity that cannot be reduced to policy proposals or political positions. There is no list of things to do. In some ways, I find that frustrating: I like lists. But I like poetry and storytelling even more. As a literary critic, I find this teaching immensely satisfying. Here is a religion for grown-ups. Here is a religion for thinkers. Here is a religion for people who want to take moral responsibility for the choices they make—and who seek intelligent help in doing so.

What these stories have to say cannot be said in any other way, in some simpler way more comfortable for highly concrete thinkers. Novelists point this out all the time. They bristle when interviewers ask them what their stories "mean," or what they think about some critic's paraphrase of their meanings. Novelists reply, in more or less hostile tones, that if they could paraphrase the meaning of the story in a sound bite then they would never have needed to spend years writing a novel. The same is true of Scripture: its authors were not "primitives" who would have written philosophy if only they knew how.

Storytelling and poetry are a rigorous way—our most robust, most durable, most sophisticated way—for engaging the paradoxes that shape human experience. What the Christian heritage of Scripture has to say is the valid core without which faith is mere sentiment and fuzzy-minded opinion. But this core cannot be extracted from the stories and the poems like walnuts from walnut shells.

Yes, there are general theological principles, like compassion and restraint and forgiveness. Do not lie, kill, steal, lust. Avoid situations where lying or stealing or killing is the only way out. But as the Dalai Lama has argued, you don't need religion to recognize the value of these moral principles: they are human universals. But universal moral principles do not provide much help at the how-to level. For help with the how-to at street level, we need the tales themselves.

And what the Jesus story demonstrates at street level, more clearly than it demonstrates anything else, is this: the biggest problems we face are not private or individual problems. The biggest, most dangerous problems we face are systemic problems. Loving your neighbor as yourself means confrontation with the socio-economic status quo. Then and now, that's dangerous. The few oppress the many so successfully because the few are both powerful and ruthless. And no power they possess is more potent than their cultural ability to define what is "realistic" or "inevitable" or "necessary."

The Dalai Lama insists that we cannot discard the conceptual bases of the different religions and yet hope to preserve the pro-social benefits in any effective form. I agree. But I'd add: neither can we discard the heritage of stories. And neither can we read those stories literally and only literally.

And so with regard to contemporary debates about Genesis and evolutionary biology: whether or not God separated the sea from the dry land on Wednesday is not the issue here. The serious issue is this: Genesis read symbolically, as a story, is dense with insight into the human condition. Read as historical or scientific fact it's nonsense. And that's a massive cultural loss of wisdom. That's doing to this ancient set of stories what roving mobs did to religious art in the 1500s and 1600s.

⁂

From a scientific perspective, no Christian stories are more problematic than the miracles of Jesus—including the central miracle of his resurrection from the dead, which I discuss as a story in *The Confrontational Wit of Jesus* [forthcoming], chapters 13 and 15. Literalists insist that these stories are factual, and they must be factual, because they serve as proof positive that Jesus is God. That is, Jesus inherits from God the Father all the absolute control over causality that God possesses as Engineer Almighty, that anthropomorphic figure in control of the Newtonian-mechanist cosmos.

Next up, then, I want to look at these miracle stories. I want to illustrate the quality of insight that is at risk in reading the Gospels literally. As the fundamentalists insist, what's at stake here is the identity of Jesus and the content of his teaching. (We agree on that much, at least.) I consider other aspects of this dispute about Jesus and his heritage in *The Confrontational Wit of Jesus* [forthcoming], especially chapter 3, on the moral imagination of Jesus, and again in *Confronting Religious Violence*, chapter 3, on religion and the social order. But I think the present context demands a frank discussion of the miracle stories—and then the closely related question of prayer.

What was Mrs. O'Malley thinking forty years ago when she prayed for my success and happiness in my chosen field? Was that simply and inevitably a call to divine tech support on my behalf? Or might it have been something else altogether, something deeply resonant within a far more sophisticated version of Christianity?

I don't know what she was thinking, of course. But her prayers are now part of my own story no matter what. And so it behooves me to have figured this out, even if only for myself.

One way or another, despite some nearly catastrophic setbacks, I am indeed happy and successful in my chosen field. Has that involved redefining "success"? Yes. You bet it has: in the eighty-year plan I formulated when I was twenty, by now I was going to be dean of a top-rated liberal arts college, if not provost of a major university. Instead I'm a mere lecturer in Medical Humanities and Bioethics, teaching writing to medical students. My contentedness today has also demanded a redefining of "my field": I'm not the major literary scholar I expected to be. I'm happy anyhow. I'm undoubtedly much happier than any provost out there. Provosts have impossible jobs. I get to sit here reading and writing for people I actually want to talk to. I'm happy in large measure because my faith has changed how I think about my own life. It has made a difference.

Mrs. O'Malley may have gotten more than she prayed for.

7

Miracles

In the eyes of many Christians—not just fundamentalists—narratives recounting Jesus' miracles must be read as factual accounts of real events. And why? Because miracles proved that Jesus was God. Miracles proved that Jesus was God because miracles proved that Jesus had a level of control over reality that only God has: just as God could reach down and turn the coffee in my mug into wine if God so desired, so also Jesus could turn enormous tanks of bathwater into wine. And so forth. Furthermore, if Jesus were not demonstrably divine, and furthermore recognized as divine by his contemporaries, then Christianity would never have arisen in the first place. But here we are, thousands of year later. *Of course Jesus could work miracles. What kind of Christian am I to question that?*

As I have already explained, acute problems follow from the assumption that God has omnipotent control over all of reality. Just for starts, it is then God's fault that reality is so replete with pain, suffering, and natural disasters.

But even aside from that argument, the claim about miracles doesn't hold. Just for starts: *at the time,* the miracle narratives would not have established the divinity of Jesus. They would not have done so for several reasons. First and foremost, it was not assumed that reality was consistent and organized according to rational and empirically discoverable mechanisms. Quite the contrary, in fact:

the dominant world view of the day held that earthly reality was programmatically and necessarily irrational, inconsistent, and arbitrary. The movements of the stars were regular, and to some limited extent the movement of the stars induced certain rough regularities, like the changes of the seasons. But all the rest of it? It was quite up for grabs. The ancient world was as comfortable ignoring regularities as we are at ignoring the exceptions and unpredictabilities of what we regard as a highly rule-governed material world.

Second, it was already widely assumed that those favored by the gods could do anything. Moses, for instances, works all kinds of miracles, but no one ever claimed he was divine. Jewish prophets worked miracles too. Such abilities were signs of divine favor or divine warrant for teachings, but not divinity itself. Even through the Middle Ages, miraculous powers were attributed to the king's touch and to a colorful array of other things. Black cats and spilt salt and ladders still have ominous associations.

What makes the miracle narratives featuring Jesus remarkable is not what these stories implicitly claim about Jesus, but what they claim about God. They make these remarkable claims within a world view which already accepted that gods—any god at all, and countless minor spirits as well—could do anything they wanted. In the world view of classical antiquity, the natural order was easily malleable. It was not rule-governed in a post-Newtonian mechanistic way. That's the cultural context of the miracle narratives. We need not accept this ancient-world physical cosmology in order to accept as true what the miracle narratives reveal *as narratives* about the moral priorities and character of the God proclaimed by Jesus.

What kind of Christian am I? Let me tell you: I'm the kind of Christian who reads what she can of biblical scholars, taking seriously the expertise that they bring to bear. And scholars contend that in the ancient world, miracle narratives are always symbolic actions. They are statements about the social, moral, and political status quo.

A Multimedia Proclamation

Ched Myers, in his commentary on the Gospel of Mark, marshals a massive body of literary evidence that the miracles do not defy the facts of physiology. They defy the structures of social and economic life in ancient Palestine. The miracles are symbolic actions embodying Jesus' revolutionary program of compassion, equality, and inclusivity.[1]

In Mark's gospel, Myers explains, Jesus does not lay out his socioeconomic-religious vision in abstrusely philosophical analyses. He acts. Jesus says very little in Mark's gospel: Mark has no "Sermon on the Mount," for instance. Instead, Jesus' actions constitute something like a multimedia presentation of his confrontational program in all of its immediate humanity. And the miracle narratives are central to this presentation.

Like other scholars, Myers explains that the miracles of Jesus were remarkably different from the miracles attributed to other figures in the ancient world. Overwhelmingly, these other miracles testify in support of the established order. In the Gospels, miracles seek to subvert the established order. That's why the Romans executed Jesus as an insurrectionist. They understood the codes. We don't, not from a distance of 2,000 years. That's why historical scholarship is so valuable. And that's why Christian humanism, beginning in the 1300s, so dramatically changed Christianity's self-understanding. These scholars—all of them devout Christians, many of them ordained clergy—began to reconstruct the cultural context of the ancient world, beginning with learning its languages.

Myers also argues that ancient-world miracle stories across the board were addressed to sociopolitical issues, not physiology. Reading them as physiology is like reading Genesis as astrophysics. It's a literal-minded category mistake. It's a mistake made by fundamentalists, of course, but it's also a mistake made by ordinary non-fundamentalist believers who have never heard sermons describing these narratives as anything *other than* historical events and proof of Jesus' divine power. And of course it's a mistake easily made by anyone at all who fails to recognize the extent to which the

---

1. Myers, *Binding the Strong Man*, 147–48.

cultural prominence of radical biblical literalism has distorted how we approach the Bible.

To understand what the miracle stories are trying to say, we need to read them as symbolic accounts. Let me begin, then, by sorting the miracle stories of the Gospel of Mark into some useful groups by symbolic category.

Symbolic Action (1): The Blind and the Deaf

Jesus repeatedly heals the deaf and the blind. Set in context, these healings approach high comedy addressed against the disciples, who consistently fail to see what Jesus is doing or to hear what he is trying to say. The blindness and deafness at stake in the story are intellectual or moral failures, not medical problems. In Mark, the only characters who see who Jesus is and hear what he is saying are the outsiders. Most of them are anonymous; many of them are women. The centrality of women in the Gospels adeptly symbolizes all the ways in which Jesus upends the usual structures of authority, even within his own community of followers.

Furthermore, healings of the blind and the deaf are part of a well-established literary tradition in Hebrew scriptures: the Messiah, when he comes, will heal our blindness and deafness to our own spiritual identity. In the book of Isaiah, for instance, it is said that the promised Messiah will heal the deaf and the blind. But there too, medical issues are not at stake. There too, the blind and the deaf do not suffer sensory deficits. They lack spiritual insight into what God commands, and why God commands it, and so they are unable to navigate reality successfully: they are hazards to themselves and to others. They cannot function successfully because they fail to orient to what is real, which is this: the welfare of each is dependent upon the welfare of all. Only the morally blind fail to see the suffering of the poor; only the spiritually deaf fail to hear the voices of the hungry, the orphaned, the widowed. That's an easy thing to say even today.

Symbolic Action (2): Paralysis

Jesus also repeatedly heals paralytics. At several points, healing of the paralyzed extends into raising the dead. The symbolic resonance of these miracles echoes out into several directions simultaneously. The first and foundational signification is socioeconomic: people are "paralyzed" by the extraordinary economic oppression imposed by Rome, an oppression aided and abetted by collaborationist religious authorities. These religious authorities subverted religious structures that had been focused on the redistribution of wealth to the poor, redirecting that money to Rome.

But that's not the whole story about Jesus' raising of paralytics and even raising the dead. These miracles also address the deeper and more intransigent problem of how oppressed populations internalize their oppression. What psychologists now call "learned helplessness" was facilitated by religious beliefs—common throughout the ancient world—equating physical disability and premature death with punishment by "the gods." That is, those who suffer are being punished. They deserve their fate. Hindu and Buddhist doctrines of "karma" involve the same dynamic, which is a near-universal human cultural assumption. It's visible among any of us in the knee-jerk reaction that asks, "what did I do to deserve this?" or in acute anxiety that a bad medical diagnosis means we are somehow "guilty" of doing something—or failing to do something—to deserve this turn of events.

In a world with this metaphysical model of physical disability and disease, it is of course socially expected—socially demanded, really—that if you have done something morally wrong or socially forbidden that then of course you will manifest this fact in physical disability. In the ancient world generally, inner reality and outer reality reflected one another with an immediacy and a vibrancy that I have repeatedly struggled to keep in mind. Consciously or not, I discovered, my knee-jerk reactions have been influenced by the radical mind-body dualism that we all inherited from the Cartesianism of the 1600s. Such dualism is inappropriate to the interpretation of ancient texts.

Let me offer an example here: if a man could not pay the ruinous taxes imposed by the Romans in an effort to force indigenous subsistence farmers off their land, his wife and children could be seized and sold into slavery. By any measure, ancient or modern, he has failed in a man's primary social responsibility to feed and to protect his own family. If such a man then fell into paralysis, that's not what we would call a "psychosomatic disorder." He's not crazy. He's not neurotic. He is expressing what has happened to him using the symbolic structures of his own society. His physical disability is perfectly normal and expected.

Symbolic Action (3): Demonic Possession

Closely related to the healings of the paralyzed is the casting out of demons. Mental illness as demonic possession? In the Gospel of Mark, Jesus encounters a man who seems to be a paranoid schizophrenic; Jesus casts demons out of this man and into a herd of pigs, who fling themselves off a cliff into the sea and drown. Is that what "really" happened? I've always objected to that story. And if that's not what "really" happened, if it didn't happen at all, then what does that say about the Gospel of Mark, where this story is told?

What it reveals about Mark, Ched Myers patiently explains, is this: the Gospel of Mark is a densely symbolic discourse from start to finish. It has an extraordinarily complex literary structure. My focus on actual pigs and an actual paranoid schizophrenics is a rudimentary, literal-minded mistake. The healing of the demoniac embodies Jesus' confrontation with what's wrong with his own society. The people are "possessed." Like the demoniac, the utterly impoverished are isolated from community; like the demoniac who lives in the graveyard, the victims of brutal colonial exploitation are the living dead. The demoniac is a complex narrative symbol for those suffering from colonial occupation. He is not a paranoid schizophrenic.

Exorcism, Myers explains, symbolically enacts the struggle between the authority of Jesus and the authority of the scribes. The scribes controlled debt in Jesus' society. The scribes created and maintained all the debt records stored in the Jerusalem temple complex. The demons cast out into the pigs are described a "legion," which is a military term, and the verb used for their being cast into the sea is the same verb used for the Egyptian troops drowned in the Red Sea during the Exodus. Ergo: Rome = Egypt; demonic possession = colonial occupation = slavery in Egypt; and so forth. The Gospel of Matthew develops Mark's equations much further, consistently portraying Jesus as in effect a new Moses.

Mark's audience would have caught the parallels just as we catch the allusions running beneath what we hear on *The Daily Show*. This miracle, like the other miracles, is addressed to our despair about our own inability to change the dysfunctional political system surrounding us. In the end, that's a despair about human nature: as a community, we just don't have what it takes. But Jesus says we are not sick nor crazy nor sinful. We are "possessed." We are "enslaved." But we can be freed, we can be liberated, just as the ancient Jews were liberated from slavery. And how did that happen? Because Moses encountered a burning bush that spoke to him. This famous scene offers a complex, theologically laden account of the power of compassion. I offer a close literary analysis of it in *Confronting a Controlling God* [forthcoming], chapter 9.

In the Gospel of Mark, as in the other Gospels, Jesus does not offer long-abstract social science analyses. Neither does he lay out complex claims in systematic theology. Except in the Gospel of John, Jesus very seldom speaks about himself. He does not claim to be God, the Son of God, or the Second Person of the Trinity. He lets his actions speak for him. He shows people the vision of human community that he has in mind by disrupting the status quo. In disrupting the status quo in these ways, he challenges conventional wisdom about who God is and how God behaves. Jesus speaks with terse authority about the difference between God's will and the goings-on of collaborationist "organized religion" of the day. The exorcisms stories, like any of the miracle stories Mark tells, are exquisitely and very complexly designed to lay out this vision.

The miracles stories in Mark are densely encoded events, Myers explains, because this Gospel was written amidst the Jewish-Roman War. Followers of Jesus refused to join Jewish guerrilla groups because they were opposed to killing anyone; but they were also notoriously opposed to Roman occupation and to the collaborationist Jewish authorities. They were caught in the middle, targets of both sides. The Gospel of Mark is a manifesto of sorts, a highly encoded manifesto.

Myers and scholars like him have explicated these cultural codes in ways that as a literary critic I find technically persuasive. It's brilliant work, a high achievement by any measure. To read Mark's Gospel literally, as a plain record of "real events," is to deprive this amazing little story of far richer, far more complex, intentionally crafted meanings. That's a tragic loss.

Symbolic Action (4): Leprosy

Myers also explains what's at stake when Jesus heals a whole array of people with diseases that left them socially ostracized. One such category of disease was "leprosy." In the ancient world, "leprosy" referred to any skin disease. It didn't mean what we know as Hansen's disease. It was a catch-all label for any skin disorder—acne, psoriasis, allergic dermatitis. Because the skin is the interface between inner world and outer world, skin diseases were particularly stigmatized as "diseases of the soul."

Jesus repeatedly touches lepers, which of course renders him "unclean" as well. (In fact, at one point in the Gospel of Mark Jesus himself is unable to enter a town where people know he has touched a leper.) Jesus also declares lepers clean. Like forgiving sin, such declarations usurped the power of central religious authorities—even though in Mark the man is told to "show himself to the priest" in order to assure the community as a whole that he has been healed. But what matters even more in the healing of lepers is this: Jesus' miracles repeatedly deconstruct the sociocultural-religious system whereby physical disability of any kind banished someone from community. Banishing "sinners" meant condemning them to radical social isolation, a banishment particularly imposed upon those with disfigured skin. Such banishment could easily translate into a solitary death on the margins.

Jesus almost always says to those he heals, "your sins are forgiven." Jesus is not saying, "yes, you have sinned, and this is your just punishment, but I'm God and because we happened to meet here today I have decided to forgive your sin." That's a misreading. Jesus is subverting the entire ancient cultural structure equating disability, disease, and injury with divine punishment.

And consider, if you will, how powerfully that subversion would have resonated for physiologically healthy people whose disability symbolically embodied their guilt over something they had done that was genuinely wrong.

Symbolic Action as Theological Claim

The healing miracles enact Jesus' confrontation with theological traditions all across the ancient world. In Jesus' rereading, God does not punish anyone. The Gospel of Mark lays out a complexly structured series of symbolic actions portraying this new theology. Mark's narrative also demonstrates that the new theology applies both to Jews and to their non-Jewish neighbors: God does not and will not smite anyone, Jew or Gentile. In this new theology, God is radically nonviolent. In this new theology, God does not give anyone leprosy, nor afflict them with blindness or with cancer or with accidents on the Interstate. That's not who God is: God's love for all of humanity is unconditional and radically inclusive. The major miracle cycle in the Gospel of Mark (4:36–8:9) offers a series of object lessons, Myers explains: first, object lessons in a new social order based on "inclusivity and compassion"; second, object lessons on a new symbolic order based on "human solidarity."[2]

We need an example here. Let's look together at one of the healing narratives to see in a particular instance how the miracle functions as a multimedia presentation of Jesus' complex political-economic-theological analysis.

One of the longest healing narratives concerns the woman with chronic vaginal bleeding—"the woman with the issue of blood," in the usual translations. She has two problems. First, a menstruating woman was ritually unclean and thus temporarily banished from the community. Her touch was thought to wreak havoc—yet

2. Ibid., 186–210.

another Jewish belief that, like attitudes toward "leprosy," was common across the ancient world. Echoes of this attitude persist in the shorthand by which women used to describe menstruation as The Curse. Women were cursed, and anything they touched while menstruating became cursed as well, whether a man or a cooking vessel or an agricultural field.

In order to render herself ritually pure again after her monthly menses, a woman (or her husband, of course) had to pay for ritual sacrifice to be offered on the woman's behalf. In the absence of this sacrifice, the household would be unable to function: it was, in effect, a tax on the mere fact of womanhood. It was a tax on the mere fact of feminine fertility. It was a tax on the source of community continuity over time, which is the ability of women to bear children. So the woman in this episode is doubly oppressed, first by social structures that were so profoundly anti-feminine, and secondly by the ways in which the collaborationist organized religion of the day capitalized upon these social structures both to enrich itself and to channel money to Rome.

In the story about this woman as told in the Gospel of Mark, she has had chronic vaginal bleeding for twelve years—one year for each of the tribes of Israel. That makes her a symbolic stand-in for all the women of Israel and all the oppression they have suffered. In the episode as Mark tells it, Jesus is en route to heal the twelve-year-old daughter of Jairus, a synagogue leader, when this woman takes the initiative.

"If I touch even his garments, I shall be made well," she says to herself (Mark 5:28). Jesus realizes someone has touched him, and so the story unfolds. It does so with far greater complexity than I need to recount here. What's fascinating to me is that the word "touch" is used four times in five verses. That which should convey curse or impurity is instead the means of healing. And all this happens on the initiative of the woman, who realizes—as the disciples still do not—that she herself must first step outside the system condemning her as ritually impure. She must dare to touch this famous rabbi Jesus. That's all she needs to do to be healed.

Jesus' response to her underscores that point: "Your faith has made you well: go in peace, and be healed of your disease" (Mark

5:34). He has not healed her. Her faith has healed her. Given the inner-reality–outer-reality literary conventions of storytelling in the ancient world, of course that means she is healed of her vaginal discharge. Her new inner or psychological reality is necessarily visible in a new outer or biological reality. That's the literary technique, common in ancient-world narratives, by which the extent of her inner change is signaled to the reader.

But the story is about something far more serious than magical control over uterine polyps or hormonal abnormalities or anything else that might cause chronic vaginal bleeding. It's about one poor and deeply ostracized woman overcoming everything that has oppressed and marginalized her, trusting that her situation will improve dramatically if only she can muster the courage to trust what Jesus has been teaching. It's about a community that rejects no one as an "abomination"—as ritually impure. And it's about an extended pattern in the Gospels of women—especially low-status women—who recognize and accept Jesus' teachings in a way that "the twelve" male disciples chronically don't.

There is more to this particular healing miracle than what I have sketched here. Jairus's twelve-year-old daughter, for instance, is thought to be dead, but given her father's faith in appealing to Jesus, she is not dead. Jesus says that she is merely asleep, and he "awakens" her. "Awakening," like "rising from the dead" is a psychologically central metaphor for a profound change in life trajectory. As the woman with the twelve-year issue of blood is the past history of Jewish women, this twelve-year-old girl is its future: through trust in the truth of what Jesus says, both of them now have a remarkably changed lives.

I'm not doing this story justice. To do it justice, this episode must be set in its full context and all of its allusive language unpacked. But we don't need to get into all that scriptural-exegetical detail to see the key point: the point of the healing miracles is not biology. These are densely symbolic actions, and it is only as symbolic actions that they still speak to us today. That symbolism is obscured for us by the massive cultural and literary differences that have arisen over 2,000 years: we need scholars like Ched Myers.

For centuries now, Christian humanism has been an intellectual tradition both sustaining such scholarship and making it as widely available as possible. Take a look, perhaps, at Myers's new book, co-written with Matthew Colwell, *Our God Is Undocumented: Biblical Faith and Immigrant Justice* (2012).

8

1960: Prayer on the Playground

In my mind's eye, I'm about eight years old. I'm on the school playground, at the edges of the jump rope area near the double doors leading into the school vestibule. And I'm looking up at an older kid. I have no idea who he is.

"Praying is just talking to yourself!" he says, in the self-righteous tone bigger kids use to tell littler kids that Santa Claus is their parents.

I didn't know what to make of this revelation. I stared up at him blankly. It had never occurred to me to wonder who I was talking to when I prayed.

We stared at each other momentarily, just long enough for my mind's eye camera to flash: he was tall and big and scary; he had a very round face and short, sandy hair. To his left, the side wall of the red-brick school; to his right, the back of the church with its high copper-green dome topped by a statue of Jesus. We are surrounded by the swirling energy of 1,200 kids confined to this wide alley and, off behind him, the somewhat wider courtyard between the school and the garage doors of the rectory.

There was no playground equipment in this space. Boys were not allowed to play with balls, lest they break a window; but girls were allowed to jump rope if someone brought a length of clothesline. As a result, bored boys plagued the edges of the jump rope area. That's where I spent these small outside intervals: I liked to watch what the talented kids could do. I loved the jump rope chants, which the surrounding circle of girls sang in unison. I was terrible at jump rope, but I was good at kicking shins: prowling boys left me alone.

Who was this kid? And what was he getting at?

He turned away. I turned inward. To whom is prayer addressed? How very odd that I'd never thought to ask—and how odder yet that the answer to such an obvious question felt so obscure.

In the Catholicism of my childhood, prayers were texts to be memorized. The "Morning Offering," which my mother had taped to the bathroom mirror for us to say to ourselves as we brushed our teeth. Grace before dinner, which we all recited together. The rosary: 53 Hail Marys, six Our Fathers, and the Apostle's Creed, interspersed here and there with the Glory Be. The Sullivan family said the rosary on their knees after dinner every night. We didn't, but I knew my mom felt guilty about that fact. She admired the Sullivans. My dad carried rosary beads in the pocket of his leather work jacket, the one the electric company logo embroidered on the chest. Dad said the rosary on the train going to work. When my Mom moved to an assisted living facility at age ninety-three, she gave me the glass rosary beads most treasured and most often used by my grandmother, Catherine Murphy. It was a solemn moment for both of us.

The rosary gave pride of place only to the Mass itself, which in those days was said (or sung) entirely in Latin. I was supposed to go to Mass every morning before school, although I only made it on time two or three mornings a week. Like my mother in relation to the Sullivans, I felt chronically inferior to kids who made it on time to Mass every day.

The school day was paced by episodes of prayer hardly less regular than the prayer cycles kept by cloistered monks and nuns. I no longer remember what we recited together at the beginning and the end of the day, but before heading home to lunch we said the Angelus, a call-and-response piece about the angel coming to Mary, and the Memorare, a prayer to the Virgin: "Remember, O most gracious Virgin Mary, that never was it known that anyone who fled to thy protection, implored thy help, or sought thy intercession was left unaided. Inspired with this confidence, I fly to thee, O Virgin of virgins, my Mother; to thee do I come; before thee I stand, sinful and sorrowful. O Mother of the Word Incarnate, despise not my petitions, but in thy mercy hear and answer me. Amen."

The Memorare always puzzled me: it sounded vaguely coercive. "See here, Mary, you have a reputation to protect . . ." On the other hand, in our unabashedly matriarchal subculture, everyone knew that the way to anyone in power was through the women in his life. Why should God be different?

After lunch we recited the Magnificat, a long poem spoken by Mary. She foretells Jesus' radical message of social and economic equality (Luke 1:46–55): the mighty put down from their thrones; the hungry fed with good things; the rich sent empty away. She also asserts her own centrality as Matriarch of the new covenant: "henceforth, all generations shall call me blessed." I was a long time recognizing how deeply the core feminism of those nuns influenced my own resilient sense of self. Women might not have mattered much in the 1950s culture surrounding me, but girls mattered to God. Mary had been a girl when all this happened. Where would we be without her?

School could stop for hours at a time for some set of formal prayers said at a particular season. Each morning during Advent, we sat on the floor in rows in the hallway to recite aloud multiple prayers and to sing multiple verses of multiple hymns yearning for the coming of the Messiah. On Friday afternoons during Lent, we spent two hours in church for Stations of the Cross. Two hours singing hymns—most of them in Latin and all of them in Gregorian chant or some variety thereof. I lost myself in that glorious music, resenting the little interludes of some nun reading something in English as she and the altar boys with their candles moved from one station to the next.

I learned to sight-read music with Gregorian notation. I don't remember learning to read words, but I do remember the utterly uncanny experience of seeing a line of music, feeling it in my throat, and hearing it in my inward ear. No one had ever told me it was possible to read music. That's another of my mind's eye snapshots:

that unbearably ugly church, this unbearably beautiful music singing itself in my head as I looked at the page.

In short, my world was full of prayers, both spoken and sung. I was slowly committing all these prayers to memory from simple fact of relentless repetition amidst a mob of older kids and adults who had themselves learned all this in the same way.

Why would God listen to any of this, I wondered. Surely God has heard it before—millions and millions of times, from time immemorial. As far as I knew, eight-year-olds had been singing these hymns on Lenten Fridays for thousands of years. God couldn't possibly be listening. What a waste of time! What a bore! God should have better things to do with his time.

Of course, all of us had heard all of this before too. Why do we do this? Why say all these same things over and over again? It seemed somehow dimly obvious that we had to be talking to ourselves—doing something to ourselves, anyhow. All these recitations of ancient poetry did something to me, that's for sure. So did all the singing of medieval music. I could feel it. What was it? I'd never asked myself that. Here was an interesting question.

What explained this boy's triumphant tone? And somehow—somehow or other—I knew that prayer was supposed to be addressed to God. But "talking to God" made no more sense than "talking to ourselves."

I did not understand. But given the importance of prayer in my world, my failure to understand felt both important and potentially dangerous. I knew this was the kind of question for which I'd get in trouble. Worse yet, I was unlikely to explain my question clearly enough to get an answer. I knew that too. My question was more like a feeling than a thought, a dark, hard area of confusion deep in my chest. A drawing back, a disengagement from the world around me that everyone else seemed to take for granted. Or to sweep aside wholesale, as this tall sandy-haired kid seemed to be doing. I said nothing because I didn't know what to say. I've been all my life finding words for these questions—and then, slowly and with great difficulty, finding answers that feel sufficient. At least for me.

As a child, I did what I always did in such situations: nothing. Nothing whatsoever. It was yet another item on my growing list of things I'd figure out for myself when I was grown up. But power of my unasked question insured that I would remember the sandy-haired boy forever afterwards.

Who are we talking to when we pray? Is "talking to" the relevant category at all? And if it's not, then what is prayer?

9

Prayer as a Creative Process

Prayer has baffled me as much as any question I've faced in writing this book—and that's saying a lot. But my difficulties make sense to me now: prayer is *prior* to the question whether or not God is real. In fact, prayer is the practice whereby one might slowly come to awareness of the reality that Christians call "God." For Christians, achieving glimpses of that awareness is roughly akin to what "enlightenment" or "nirvana" is for Buddhists. As a result, prayer is central to the human experience that has sustained Christian tradition for 2,000 years. The illusory conflict between religion and science will never be resolved until the truth-claims made by praying or appropriate to the experience of prayer have been sorted out.

Here's the key assumption shaping my approach to the question of prayer: it seems to me that an accurate understanding of who God is follows from the human experience of God's elusive Presence as discovered in praying. Let me repeat that: who we think God is follows from what we experience in prayer. Theological and doctrinal claims about God are derived from the primary experience of prayer. Praying is, as it were, the "empirical" basis of the whole tradition.

This is a big claim. I'm taking sides here in a very ancient, contentious debate between the well-ordered priestly class of institutional leaders and the unruly, disreputable tribe labeled "mystics" or "prophets." Institutional insiders are far more likely to insist the heritage of Scripture, doctrine, and dogma together provides a set of immediately valid propositional claims—claims that they control and no one else can question.

I disagree. To my mind, the basis of the faith is the human encounter with the sacred, not the inherited array of propositional claims, no matter how august. The God who will be what he will be cannot be confined to propositional, systematic theology from the ancient world.

So I'll risk disapproval from the institutional types. After all, poets are always lumped in with prophets and mystics. We are a suspect lot, the whole bunch of us. As I see it, then—as the mystic-poetic-prophetic half of the ancient debate sees it—Scripture is the narrative and poetic record of classical-era masters in the spiritual art of praying. Like theology itself, Scripture is secondary to the immediate experience of prayer. But in its narrative and poetic prowess, in its sheer literary ability to evoke what the experience of Presence feels like, Scripture comes far closer to the primary experience of God than theology ever will.

I understand now why I put off writing about prayer until last or nearly last in the ten years of work on this series of little books. First I had to work my own way through all my own objections to what institutionalized Christianity has become in the span of 2,000 years. Until I had faced—and faced down—all of those doubts and all of those gut-deep suspicions, I could not begin to engage critically with my own experience of prayer.

In short: writing about praying has been even more daunting than daring to write about Jesus. All I can say here is what I will say again when I grapple with the possibility that the radical Religious Right has betrayed the historical Jesus of Nazareth: I'd rather risk being wrong than fail to figure out where I stand personally on anything this important.

My goals in the next several chapters are simple. First I want to suggest that there are reasonable grounds for distinguishing between prayer and furry-minded magical thinking. Second, I want to sketch a useful framework that might help you to make sense of other sources on this topic.

There is a huge array of other sources on the topic of prayer. What's missing from the lineup, it seems to me, is an overview written for complete outsiders, and furthermore an overview that does not attempt to drag outsiders inside. I've said this before and in other ways, but let me say it again here: I don't care whether you pray. I'm not trying to talk anyone into any form of religious observation. But I am trying to explain what committed Christians are doing that can be made perfectly comprehensible even to nonbelievers. I don't understand first hand what happens in chemistry labs either. I never did college-level chemistry. But I'm not a science illiterate: I do have a general sense of what's going on. I'm offering the equivalent here, and nothing more. That's a promise.

In what follows, then, I will try to sidestep the jargon, the allusions, and above all the assumptions of insider talk among Christians. I will speak as plainly as the topic allows about a single-pointed question: is prayer self-deceptive "talking to yourself" or magical thinking, neurotic nonsense? Or might there be some "there" there?

I think there is something real going on. Or at least there might be something real. There can be. It all depends.

The Problem of Public Prayer

Let me begin by admitting something obvious. Public prayer—what one hears in church on Sunday—can be a colossal problem. If all you know about prayer is what you have heard in random churches on Sunday, then you may have very good reason to be extraordinarily skeptical. Public worship ought to be a high performance art: subtle, passionate, poetic, aesthetically sound in its dramatic arc, and above all evocative of the elusive inward encounter with the sacred. It can be glorious. It can be deeply moving.

But sometimes it's not. Just for a start, public prayer often talks about God with wildly inappropriate confidence. In such prayers, "God" comes across as a rich and elderly uncle living in a distant city. We talk to him loudly and in forcefully declamatory tones because after all these years he has gotten a little deaf. And he is very far away, on a speaker phone perhaps—although he never says anything himself.

Dear Uncle God likes to be flattered. He could solve all of our problems if he wanted to, although of course we can't complain that he hasn't. We can't even admit our expectation that he should have by now. We never tell him what we are really thinking about his refusal to rescue suffering humanity for lo! these thousands of years: we don't want to alienate the old coot. One of these days he might actually come through for us.

Worse yet, we remember all the ancient stories about what a temper he had years ago. It's wise to be circumspect about dear old Uncle God. Honest, angry questions about tragedy and innocent suffering all too often go unspoken: hush, not a word. Not in church.

If the flaming irrelevance of such public worship leaves you feeling just a bit toasted, then your heart is in the right place. That mix of groveling and grandiosity drives me crazy too. Intellectually serious believers spend a lot of time grousing to one another about how hard it is to find a good church. The only group more disgruntled are intellectually serious clergy. They are burned to a crisp by hostile, infantile congregants who are desperate to enlist both the congregation and the pastor in supporting their own neuroses, repressions, and refusals. Thoughtful, generous, well-educated clergy are overworked, underpaid, and seldom appreciated for doing a remarkably difficult job. Like teachers, most leave the field within five years.

I realized at one point that the church is all too much like the university. What a great teacher can do is extraordinary. But good teachers are routinely ground into sawdust by hostile, indifferent students. Good students, in turn, are alienated by teachers who are incompetent, burned out, hostile, or all of the above. Hostile, indifferent students and hostile, indifferent faculty poison the atmosphere for everyone else. Administrators often have not a clue and could care less. It all goes downhill from there.

But in the university as in the church, there are extraordinary bright spots of resistance: the great student who keeps the great teacher going; the great teacher who inspires a student in life-changing ways; central administrators who care passionately about

funding and nurturing everything that makes possible both exu-
berant teaching and engaged learning. That happens too. It happens
all the time.

In short: real Christianity, like real education, takes place
against the grain of human alienation, hostility, egotism, and in-
competence. As I will never give up on the idea of the university,
despite its obvious dysfunctions, so I will never give up on the idea
of the church. Real classrooms, like real Christian community, may
be a phenomena that appears only transiently, like certain rare
wildflowers in the woods. But if we want such flowers of human
creativity and compassion, we need to protect and maintain the
habitat—the bricks-and-mortar habitat, the face-to-face habitat,
where real people gather to share questions, to listen openly, and
to engage with inherited wisdom. It seems to me, looking both at
churches and at universities, that something akin to purple loose-
strife or garlic mustard are infesting these habitats. And yet, we'd be
fools to abandon crucial habitats just because they are threatened
by invasive, opportunistic weeds.

I will one day have sharp words on this topic with the archangel in charge of human-resource deployment. Why, in the name of
all that's holy, do good and thoughtful folks, lay and ordained alike,
have such a terrible time finding one another? Pending whatever
that archangel might tell me, I have no explanation—despite years
of listening to the deep pain and bitter frustration of good friends
on all sides. All I can say is this: real Christian community flour-
ishes when these good people find one another. It happens. Never
easily, mind you. But it happens.

And so: quite aside from whatever nonsense you may have
encountered in the past, prayer is a serious topic. It deserves serious, open-minded consideration.

Prayer is ubiquitous in human cultures, just as religion itself
is ubiquitous. Underneath the nonsense of so much public prayer
there is something remarkably real. Only the greatest of pastors and
liturgists know how to evoke communal openness to the elusive,
enigmatic Presence of the sacred at the far edges of our inward pe-
ripheral vision. No matter how badly public prayer is performed
in any given church on Sunday morning, then, cultural history

suggests that prayer is a centrally important dimension of the human experience.

Historically speaking, communal prayer is also the art that mothered all the other arts. Music, poetry, painting, storytelling, sculpture: they all began in the service of communal worship. The earliest instances we have reveal that unequivocally. The arts have grown into their own separate and secular cultural activities, but their origins within religion testify plainly that religion is an interdisciplinary art form. It is not an obsolete version of science, just as it is not an incompetent version of philosophy. It is an art, or it is a tradition within the arts. It is a community of people gathering to engage with that tradition and with the truths and the insights it has to offer—truths and insights that cannot be expressed in some simpler, less densely artistic ways. Jesus was a storyteller. If God had wanted to become incarnate as a philosopher or a systematic theologian, then I assume that God could have done so.

My question, then, is rudimentary: what is actually going on when believers pray? Or more precisely, I suppose: what should be going on? What is prayer?

Prayer and the Arts

To whom is prayer addressed? That is a first-order question. And that was the issue at stake when I was confronted by an older classmate there at the edge of the jump rope area. Behind his challenging assertion that prayer is talking to ourselves stood an obvious assumption. This assumption permeates every Christian guide to prayer that I've ever browsed: prayer is talking to God.

That is not the case. Or at least not literally. It is a metaphor. Prayer is like talking to someone. Over time—over centuries—the metaphor has felt so brilliantly effective for so many people that "talking to God" has become a symbolic complex. The claim that we can "talk to God" offers a small, psychologically vivid way to gesture toward an enormously complex array of spiritual insights into the relationship between the human and the sacred.

Perhaps an analogy will help to illustrate the point I'm trying to make. The idea that prayer is "talking to God" functions something like a stage convention: in church (or in private prayer) we "talk to God" just as theatergoers or film viewers agree that the action on stage or screen is "really happening."

The action on stage or screen certainly is "real," but it is not the same reality as ordinary life. It is not "real" in the same way that our own immediate experience is real. The action played out before us is a dimension of reality that we only experience in theaters or equivalent spaces. The reality of this dimension is attested to by our tears, our pounding hearts, our heartache as we sit in the darkened theater, watching the screen or the stage. The wisdom we acquire from dramatic productions is as potent as any in our lives. Novels and poetry provide a similar access: most of us have set aside a novel or a volume of poetry because we need to sit quietly with our own inward response to what we have just read.

Literary theorists have struggled for thousands of years to explain the depth and the power of our response to literature. The world of the story is not the "real" world. Why then do we react as we do? That's why Plato was so suspicious of storytellers: he did not trust the tribe of poets and storytellers to use this uncanny power for the purposes of the state. Dictators know this: totalitarian states brutally silence poets, songwriters, dramatists, novelists, and filmmakers. They are also driven to control religion or to adopt a religious guise themselves: they want to get their hands on the extraordinary power of prayer, especially communal prayer.

Totalitarian dictators are drawing on an ancient playbook when they do so. In the eighth century, for instance, the newly crowned emperor Charlemagne seized control of Christian worship with great speed and devastating consequences. In *Saving Paradise* (2008), as brilliant a bit of historical theology as I have ever read, Rita Nakashima Brock and Barbara Ann Parker trace a direct line from his liturgical changes to the pseudo-theological justifications for crusades and inquisitions. As they explain, Charlemagne's brutally violent God offered theological warrant for human political violence. I discuss that in detail in *Confronting Religious Violence*, chapter 8, because the influence of Charlemagne is visible even today. It's painfully clear every time some televangelist blames some tragedy—anything from 9/11 to Sandy Hook—upon the fact that

American civil rights are displeasing to God, as are separation of church and state, or our cultural traditions of social inclusivity and mutual respect.

And so: prayer is not literally addressed to God just as what's happening on screen is not literally taking place. It is "taking place"—no doubt about that. Screenwriters, actors, producers, set designers, camera folks: lots of people work very hard for years to make any film, and that doesn't count the years prior to that wherein each gained the necessary professional skill. But what happens on screen is not literally happening. In the same way, prayer is not literally "talking to God." But if you refuse outright to consider the imaginative reality of the artistic convention, then you exclude yourself from the long conversation trying to explain this commonplace and culturally central human experience.

If prayer uses words at all, then it is symbolic speech. What is "addressed" to God are not sentences made of up of clauses. What is "addressed to God" is pure introspection: the wordless self-awareness taught by mindfulness meditation. That same self-awareness can also be carried along within a repeated mantra, or an inherited text like the fifty-three Hail Marys of the rosary, or the stream of what psychologists call "self-talk" (such as "Don't let it be malignant"). Nonetheless: the introspective state of consciousness is the prayer. Not the words. At most, at best, the words incarnate and express the introspection. The words evoke the inward experience, which remains itself beyond words. Tradition insists that the prayerful encounter with God is always beyond words.

Here's the bottom line as I see it: prayer is an introspective creative process seeking spiritual and personal growth through changes in self-awareness. The key change in self-awareness, according to the best Christian teachers I've found, is becoming self-aware of the Presence within consciousness of that which we experience as by definition beyond human comprehension. God, in short. But not Uncle God on his speaker phone far away. Not God the Superhero leaning his elbows on the railing around some celestial balcony, looking down on us. Not God the Engineer Almighty ignoring the tech-support requests we send desperately seeking his intervention. Something far more intimate, far more elusive. Something both incredibly near the strings of the heart, yet simultaneously so far beyond comprehension that human cultural traditions have named it in innumerable ways.

All of these names are true. And none of them are. Some things can't be named directly—and that's why we have the arts. That's where the arts originate: in the drive to express what cannot be expressed in simple, direct, literal ways. And that's why we have religious traditions. Christianity is a culturally specific thematic collection of densely symbolic artworks all focused on one particular category of human experience: the encounter with what I have come to call "God."

In prayer I have encountered love so vast I can only describe it by analogy to a "cosmic force" of the kinds physicists describe. I have encountered compassion so inclusive I want to call it something like the gravitational constant. I am speaking poetically, reaching for analogies to what I encounter as beyond description. These are merely the best analogies I can come up with. However it might be named—no matter what analogy works best for you or for anyone else—I have discovered that each of us, all of us, all of us everywhere, are cherished so completely that in this moment of spiritual apprehension the moral significance of my own life felt beyond question. The moral significance of every life felt beyond question, even the lives of butterflies and protozoa and black holes and the sand on the beach. Or as Gerard Manley Hopkins put it, "The world is charged with the grandeur of God"—"charged" in the double sense of permeated by and called to account by. Do we know who we are? Are we living in accord with our own fullest identity? Maybe for sand or for butterflies that's an easy question: they have few if any choices. For me it is a question.

But let me repeat: tradition insists that this elusively enigmatic Presence is also far greater than anything anyone can say. That humility is bedrock. Even "love" or "compassion" is only a glimpse. It's the closest we can come to naming what we have glimpsed. But even this glimpse does not entirely make sense: look at how much suffering there is in the world. How can "cosmic love" be reconciled with the dynamic character of a cosmos in which stars and species and we ourselves are all doomed to die? When we encounter love and deep sustaining compassion for our inescapable suffering, we simultaneously intuit the Presence of something overwhelmingly more—something far more than we will ever understand.

The intensity of that paradox has elicited thousands of years of extraordinary art.

~

There is much that might be said on this topic. That's obvious. If you want to pick up from what I've said here, please read Lewis Hyde, *The Gift* (1979), on creativity, and then the first half of Richard Kearney, *Anatheism* (2010), on God as an elusive stranger whom we welcome or ignore as we choose. And then either David Steindl-Rast, *Gratefulness, the Heart of Prayer* (1984), a very accessible book, or Laurence Freeman, *Jesus: The Teacher Within* (2000), which is rather more complex. But we need to move on here. I want to stay focused on the question at hand, which is sanely sorting out the complicated relationship between scientific research as a complex human activity and religion as a complex human activity.

To that end, I turn next to a simple, secular, introspective exercise that medical science and neuroscience have both studied in considerable detail: mindfulness mediation. Mindfulness meditation has religious correlates, of course. In fact, the secular variety is both quite recent and transparently honest about its derivation from religious practice. Nonetheless, these secular exercises and scientific studies of practitioners offer a useful and I hope easily shared starting point from which to explain both Christian mediation and other varieties of prayer practice in the Christian tradition.

What are people doing when they pray? Prayer is an introspective exercise: believers are centering their attention in particular ways. The consequences of that centering have been rigorously studied. Let's begin there.

10

Mindfulness Meditation and the Brain

In the last fifty years or so, researchers in a variety of disciplines have documented the fact that prayer can change our brains. In fact, mindfulness-based stress reduction (MBSR) has now moved into the medical mainstream. It's recognized as a valid way to lower blood pressure, reduce stress hormones, treat chronic physical pain, alleviate depression or anxiety, improve concentration, treat OCD or ADHD, and so forth. In 1975, Herbert Benson, MD, a cardiologist at Harvard, dubbed this physiological change "the relaxation response" in his book by that title. Physiologically speaking, the relaxation response is the opposite of the fight-or-flight stress response. It reverses all the complicated physical reactions that stress evokes.

And that's not all. Subsequently, and with newer technologies like the fMRI, neuropsychologists have mapped in considerable detail how mindfulness meditation practice evokes changed patterns in neural activation and measures of concentration. These changes are empirically demonstrable after even minimal training in basic meditation technique. Further studies of highly skilled meditators have revealed their remarkable control over patterns of neural activation.

Sharon Begley has explained all this in *Train Your Mind, Change Your Brain* (2008). She and Richard Davidson later collaborated on *The Emotional Life of Your Brain* (2012), a detailed account of Davidson's research at the University of Wisconsin, Madison. The key finding of all this research is easily explained: the mind can change the brain. The brain is more like a muscle than a computer: where and how we direct our attention changes neural functioning in a variety of well-documented ways. The brain, like many other body parts, will change depending upon how it is used. Our famously flexible behavior would not be half so flexible if the brain were not capable of adapting to the demands placed upon it by the organism generally.

That sounds like such common sense! Nonetheless, I was at first astounded by this research. That's because for most of the twentieth century, scientists insisted that the adult brain is fixed. We are born with all the brain cells we would ever have, it used to be said: it's downhill from there. And in parallel ways, the adult personality was portrayed as essentially immutable—determined by experience in very early childhood. But scholarly opinion on the immutability of the adult brain has quite dramatically changed. As Begley wittily explains, assuming that the brain is fixed is like assuming that muscle tone is fixed. Muscle tone will be fixed, of course—in the absence of exercise. But as even octogenarians can gain physical strength, even octogenarians still have brain stem cells churning out new neurons. The issue at stake, whether for muscles or for brains, is exercise.

Mindfulness-based stress reduction exercises are common-place teachings in major religious traditions East and West alike. Such teachings go back thousands of years. The exercise is universal, just as singing or painting or playing musical instruments are universal. As Benson documented very nicely in 1975, every major religious tradition teaches this practice. Furthermore, despite important theological differences, every major tradition teaches a remarkably similar physical technique.

"Just Physiology?"

In effect, then, these many different religious traditions each offer spiritual interpretations of the physiological relaxation response that Benson documented. Does that mean that religious meditation is "nothing but physiology"? And that we'd be better off dropping this religious flimflam and admitting it's *just* physiology?

That's a coherent position to take. I disagree, but I am not inclined to argue with anyone taking that position. Of course, reducing meditation practice to mere physiology does not explain the scientific finding that meditation practice leaves people both feeling more compassionate and more inclined to act compassionately. Perhaps that too will one day be explained away as a mere physiological by-product, perhaps a by-product selected for by evolutionary pressures shaping religious traditions. I have no trouble with that possibility either. I'm sure that physiological mechanisms do exist somewhere, and maybe someday some clever neuroscience team will figure that out.

But I still think it makes sense to consider that as religions have grown up around this fact of our physiology, religious traditions have expanded and explored the human significance of this experience. Those explorations are wise and remarkably sophisticated. They are a cultural treasure beyond value.

For instance, in complex cultural ways, religions have encouraged people to take the time and to invest the energy needed to become adept at meditating. Until just a few decades ago, meditation practice had been sustained by religious organizations for thousands of years. Meditation practice is a clear example of the wisdom that religions sustain—if and only if authentic religions are neither discredited (or "exterminated") by dogmatic scientism nor outflanked by fundamentalist exploitation. Or both.

The religious teachings surrounding meditation practice are complex. They are also deeply situated within the world view of the culture within which each religion originated. The differences among them are serious and must not be minimized. To do so is to lose all the fine-grain detail that makes the different portraits of our inner landscape so remarkably fascinating. Consider this analogy: all painters use paint or something like paint; all writers use language. That doesn't mean we can ignore differences in artistic traditions or literary traditions. To do so would be an extraordinary loss. The same holds for religion. Each teaches some variety of meditation practice, but the practice itself is part of a rich tradition situating such experiences within a complex, highly symbolic world view.

How It Works

The core physical action at the heart of meditation practice is quite simple. Here's how it goes. Sit comfortably. Close the eyes or let the gaze rest on some unchanging object. Attend to the in-breath and the out-breath. If a distracting thought appears in consciousness (as it most assuredly will), return to paying attention to the breath.

The goal is not to stop all distracting thoughts. That's an impossible goal. The benefit of the practice arises not from stopping distractions but rather from repeatedly beginning again to attend to the breath. It seems to me that meditation is in that way something like weightlifting: the goal of the beginning weightlifter is not to hold a weight up in the air for twenty minutes twice a day. The weightlifter hoists the weight, lowers it, and repeats the sequence. So also, in meditation, the meditator over and over again "lifts" the conscious attention from the distraction back to the breath. By analogy, the recurrence of distracting thoughts is like the lowering of the weight—except that distraction arises spontaneously. It is as if the weightlifter's weight lowered itself.

To diminish the frequency of these distractions, many traditions suggest inwardly repeating a word or phrase. This repeated word or phrase—the "mantra"—can be anything at all. Benson quotes a literary critic saying that Alfred Lord Tennyson repeated his own name. Both Christian and Buddhist traditions have a wide array of traditional words or phrases that one might use. Each of these traditional words or phrases also carries a lot of theological and cultural freight for guiding the meditator toward particular interpretations of the experiences that arise within meditation exercise. The more I have learned about that interpretive freight, the more distracting I've found all of it.

But that may be me: I'm a writer; I focus on words. As a thinker, I'm also strongly systematic and concept-oriented. I need to keep conceptual vocabulary out of my way when I meditate, and all mantras are, in the end, allusion to theological concepts. Once in a while I use a mantra simply as a barrier to that incessant flow of words through my consciousness. But on the whole I'm better off centering my attention deep within my body. Search online for "body scan meditation" and you will find countless recordings walking you through this kind of meditation practice.

If you are a beginner, start with the body scan. Do a forty-five-minute version at least once a day for six months before you try anything else—including trying to decide if meditation is all nonsense. That might sound like a big commitment. But compare it to what would be required if you were trying to learn to play a violin. If you don't know the first thing about music, if you have never played another stringed instrument, it might take six months of work to play even a simple tune without the dreadful squawks and squeals of the beginning violinist.

In MBSR training, the story ends with following the breath and remaining centered in bodily self-awareness. I've done this secular version meditation off and on since Benson's book first came out in 1975. Not regularly, I confess, just as I don't regularly get as much physical exercise as I should. But I have stopped again and started again often enough to be convinced that forty-five to ninety minutes a day of mindfulness meditation, like equivalent time on the treadmill, makes a remarkable difference. I'm saner and more productive. Ninety minutes a day is something like ten times more effective than forty-five minutes. I don't pretend to understand why that is the case. But that's my experience, and that's what master practitioners teach.

Mindfulness Practice and Church Authority

Why didn't I persist with meditation practice after reading Benson in 1975? Let me tell you why: the nuns. The nuns had told us about this kind of praying when I was in high school: it is regarded as the purest and the most powerful form of prayer. They cautioned that this kind of praying is appropriate only for monks, nuns, and priests. Even for them, meditation is undertaken only under close professional supervision. No one should attempt this at home, we were told.

There are two very solid reasons for that traditional caution. One is the power of our own unconscious stuff, which will surely rise into awareness. Religious craziness can follow. As Laurence Freeman insists, if you think God is talking to you as you meditate, ignore it. If you think you are being given a vision or something is "happening," ignore it. Odds are overwhelming that this is your own unconscious stuff coming to the surface.

If some change is called for in your life, Freeman explains—if you keep feeling "I should quit that job, I should quit that job," don't simply attribute that feeling to "God" and email your resignation. If quitting is the right thing for you to do, that fact will also become evident to you in all the ordinary ways that people recognize such facts. Test the validity of the urge in all of the usual ways. And if you are deeply troubled by feelings or urges that surface repeatedly in meditation practice, then get help from a therapist. Such cautious testing is called "discernment." I do a short summary of classic discernment practices in the last section of *Selling Ourselves Short* (2004).

Meditation practice does make a big difference in life, Freeman insists. But it makes a difference only indirectly and only over time: we discover ourselves on a day-to-day basis more patient, more compassionate, more open. We become less reactive, less judgmental, less anxious or depressed. We become more deeply focused and more freely creative in whatever we undertake.

Freeman is obviously opposed to the kind of "talking to God" practices described by T. M. Luhrman in *When God Talks Back: Understanding the American Evangelical Relationship with God* (2012). Luhrman is an anthropologist; she closely and quite thoughtfully studied several Vineyard Christian Fellowship congregations. They are charismatic Pentecostalists, an evangelical movement beginning in the early twentieth century. Charismatic Pentecostalism carries to extraordinary lengths the classic "pietist" emphasis on one's individual relationship with God. Some such groups are politically quite conservative; others are at the very forefront of the "emergent church" movement, taking seriously Jesus' teachings about inclusivity and concern for the poor. Either way, however, they tend to disregard the ancient warnings that Freeman repeats so bluntly.

For easy access to this ancient mystical tradition and all of its hard-nosed advice, go read Evelyn Underhill, *Mysticism: A Study in the Nature and Development of Man's Spiritual Consciousness* (1911). This classic work went through dozens of editions in its day, and now it's widely available as a free e-book. Her language is a bit dated in some ways; but when I first read it years ago, I was nonetheless startled by the psychological sophistication and acute religious skepticism on display in what she quoted from her array of ancient and medieval mystics. We are clearly not the first generation to be suspicious of pious nonsense. And so, as much as I enjoyed Luhrman's quite nuanced and sympathetic analyses of her Vineyard congregations, thousands of years of Christian wisdom would insist that these good people are playing with fire. Maybe for some people, the minimal safeguards Luhrman describes are quite sufficient. But I think that vulnerable people might be badly injured by such teachings.

Freeman's shrewd and ancient wisdom is only half of the story why the nuns made such a deal about meditation practice as a powerful but forbidden practice. I was decades recognizing how— within strict limits imposed by an extraordinarily controlling and conservative cardinal in his mansion downtown—they were trying to alert us to cutting-edge developments in Christian spirituality. If we were never to do this unless we became nuns and even then only under close institutional supervision, why tell us at all? To alert us, I now realize, to the renewed interested in meditation practice led by figures such as Freeman's teacher, another Benedictine monk named John Main. Despite institutional opposition, he began teaching meditation practice to ordinary laypeople in 1975. The nuns in my high school—a cutting-edge group if ever there were one—undoubtedly had been introduced to the practice before books about it and classes became available to the general public.

Institutional leaders could be suspicious of meditation practice not from a healthy regard for the power of the unconscious but rather because gains in healthy and solid self-awareness can make anyone far less complaint with stupid stuff in the cultural generally—and in the church itself. As Laurence Freeman points out, "institutional religious leaders have discouraged contemplative experience for the many. It creates too many prophets and raises too many people with the authority of real holiness."[1] As I said, Freeman is both a globally famous meditation teacher and a Benedictine monk. He is the director of the World Community for Christian Meditation (wccm.org). His dialogue with the Dalai Lama, *The Good Heart: A Buddhist Perspective on the Teachings of Jesus* (1996), reveals the complexity and the density of the theology behind meditation practice in the two traditions. The Benedictine movement predates the papacy by centuries: these monks rightly claim a prior and independent authority. If you recognize the institutional codes, Freeman's remark about official suppression of meditation practice has a significantly defiant edge to it.

And I'm taking Freeman's defiant edge a bit further out when I insist that who we think God is *follows from* what we experience in prayer. As believers have insisted for thousands of years, theological and doctrinal claims about God are *derived from* the primary experience of prayer. Praying is, as it were, the "empirical basis" of the whole tradition. Certain leaders of the institutional church—Protestant and Catholic alike—might reply that the basis of the whole tradition is divine self-revelation through Scripture and through doctrine, both of which are safely under the control of authorities.

I disagree with that. And if that's heresy, I'm guilty. But there are a whole lot of us out here thinking this way. I think it's high time we spoke up in ways that are broadly accessible to outsiders.

Why I Hesitated

The revival of meditation practice in the Christian tradition was only beginning to get underway when Benson's book appeared in 1975: that's the same year that John Main first began publicly teaching meditation practice to laypeople. Laurence Freeman's comment would not appear in print for another twenty-five years. In the

1. Freeman, *Jesus the Teacher Within*, 130

meantime—in 1975—the nuns' sharp cautions echoed in my mind. Even after reading Benson, I felt that I was playing with fire—a fire I did not understand.

Timothy Leary was from Harvard too, after all: there was lots of casual experimenting with the mind and the brain in the 1960s and 1970s. I had a good college friend who fried his brains with LSD, and I've always been haunted by what happened to Lou. I stayed away from street drugs. Perhaps meditation practice was just as risky. The 1960s and 1970s were replete with "consciousness-raising" practices that struck me as self-delusional. Perhaps the good nuns, who had so often proved trustworthy in my life, should be trusted on this matter.

I remained both skeptical and cautious, even as my friends starting forking over several months' rent for Transcendental Meditation workshops. Soon the Rackham Graduate Library at the University of Michigan was peppered with students sitting cross-legged on the floor between rows of bookcases, taking meditation breaks from whatever they were reading. I tip-toed around them physically just as I tip-toed around the concept of meditation practice. When I felt inward changes from meditation practice on my own, as I certainly did, I would stop. I would stop for months or even years at a time, until the daily experience of ordinary stress slowly drew me back into the solace of this silent, attentive sitting. And then I would stop again. And so the cycle would repeat.

In short: I had far too many doubts about the essential toxicity of Christianity to pursue this ancient Christian practice in any serious way, even if in these apparently secularized forms. I have slowly resumed meditation practice as I have slowly worked through all my own gut-deep questions about Christianity by writing this series of little books. That has taken me more than a decade. And then, at last, in my mid-60s I took a straight secular MBSR course. I did so after reading Begley's book *Train Your Brain*, and then her book with Davidson *The Emotional Life of Your Brain*. And I did so in part, I confess, because taking such a course struck me as a reasonable research project for anyone writing about prayer and about the troubled relationship between science and religion.

The familiarity of what I learned astounded me. It shined a light backward through my life, illuminating and interrelating a whole series of experiences. As a steeply intuitive asthmatic introvert, I'd been centering inwardly like this all my life, monitoring my breathing, slowly calming down, noticing my breaths become deeper and more steady. That's how people like me recover from sensory-social overload. What I found at such moments had never aligned with what the church called "God," and so I called it "imagination" or "the sources of imagination" if I called it anything. Mostly I didn't call it anything. No name seemed remotely adequate. It didn't need a name. The silence and I were comfortable with one another. We had been comfortable with one another for as long as I could remember. Except that even saying "we" feels like naming what I do not want to name. For most of my life, I let such experiences be what they were, lightly, and as it were *reverently*. So to speak.

God is patient, of course. Or persistent? Tradition cautions about that too.

11

Meditation, Imagination, and God

In religious meditation, the story about meditation practice begins at the point where secular MBSR practice falls silent: what happens once you master this technique? In the East and West alike, there are thousands of years of teachings on two key issues regarding what happens next—and what it means.

First, every time a distraction arises, I see what is distracting me. Over time, patterns arise. These patterns are undeniable. They are revealing. That evokes a significant change in consciousness right there. Psychotherapy is often based on becoming conscious of this ongoing stream of consciousness and all of its obsessions. But Western secular psychotherapy has its roots in religion: Christian spiritual counsel or "care of the soul" goes back thousands of years. The assumption behind prayer is that healthy people who have both personally supportive community and reasonable access to this ancient wisdom can cope successfully with whatever meditative introspection brings to the surface.

Furthermore, and by analogy to weightlifting, over time the distractions one encounters become weightier. I have been faced repeatedly with what I would rather not face. That too can force a significant change in consciousness. What am I to do with what these weightier distractions showed me? How am I to do so? Where do I turn for the wisdom I need? What is my own unconscious stuff and what is insight into the decadent symbolic systems of the culture all around me?

That's never an easy question. Different religious traditions offer quite different advice about how to interpret and how to respond to what surfaces. Such advice is based upon different cultural and theological interpretations of the human condition. Each tradition also has its own symbolic systems and narrative resources for expressing and transmitting these insights over time. But every tradition, each in its own way, recognizes the reality of such psychological dynamics as projection, denial, defense mechanisms, misplaced ambition, egotism, and potent negative emotions such as jealousy, envy, lust, greed, anger, or aggression.

(In this context, I should to point out that there is a significant strand within Christian spiritual teachings that can be sexually obsessed. Such repression came into the tradition from ancient-world Neoplatonism, especially in its Gnostic subvarieties. Gnosticism was radically dualist; it was extraordinarily hostile to the body, which it regarded as a vile trap for the pure spirit. In the sexual act, the purely cerebral spirit gives way to a powerfully embodied sensation. As a result, sex was suspect. Sex moved us in the wrong direction altogether. But Gnosticism was a hugely influential aspect of the culture surrounding early Christianity. Under pressure from this cultural context, scholars explain, sexual renunciation replaced kosher regulations as a marker of community boundaries. I tell this story in more detail in *Confronting Religious Denial of Gay Marriage,* chapter 5. It's quite a tale.)

Changes in Self-Awareness

There is a second major issue to consider under the heading of "what happens next," what happens after meditation technique has been mastered sufficiently to start messing around with consciousness. Something happens to consciousness or within consciousness that goes far beyond throttling back our physiological stress responses or improving our ability to concentrate. We go from being aware (a sentient capacity we share with squirrels) to becoming increasingly self-aware.

We become increasingly conscious, more continuously conscious, of the entire stream of consciousness flowing through our minds. That gives us something like better access to the full depth and richness of our own awareness of the world. This deep, rich self-awareness is an essential prerequisite to creativity of any kind, in any field of endeavor: the more delicately self-aware we are, the more easily we become aware of our own hunches and insights and solutions to problems. Without that self-awareness, the creative process never gets going in the first place.

Given my overarching claim that Christianity—and possibly religion across the board—is anchored in the creative process, I have a lot at stake here. As I figured out this much about prayer, I figured out something else as well: I understood why I kept being drawn into meditative prayer practices even during the decades when I kept a hostile distance from "organized religion" of any kind. Meditation practice feeds my creativity. It kept me going through the difficult years when my children were young, even though I backed away abruptly each time this inexplicable Presence loomed too large on the periphery of my awareness.

I want to explain, then, what I mean by "self-aware." I want to do so without getting bogged down in technical jargon from any of the relevant academic disciplines. I do appreciate all the nuance I'm losing by avoiding academic jargon, but I think the core reality here is profoundly familiar to all of us already. I'm not trying to convert anyone, and I'm not trying to compete with neuropsychologists or monks or anyone else who has spent a lifetime meditating seriously or studying meditation scientifically (or both). I'm simply struggling to understand my own life and to be morally accountable for the life I am living. And so I'll use a simple analogy: talk radio.

The All Talk All the Time Broadcast

Some years ago a radio station in Chicago changed its format, beginning to boast "All Talk, All the Time." The first time I heard that tag line, I almost ran the car up onto the curb. That's it! That's what it feels like! I have between my ears my very own All Talk All the Time radio station. I have in my head a radio station that

I can't turn off. Its content can vary from something like the best of National Public Radio to something like the most embarrassing self-absorbed fact-free ranting you can possibly imagine. At most I can turn down the volume. Sometimes. Briefly. But turn it off? No. Except very briefly, for no more than a minute or two at a time, while I'm meditating.

Broadcasts can wake me up at three in the morning. The volume can be cranked up so high I can't imagine how my husband can continue snoring softly next to me in bed. I do not understand how I can be so fantastically alert at such an hour. I have always been very slow to awaken—but not when that radio starts blaring. It jolts me awake with some regularity.

Sometimes I awaken amidst a news broadcast about whatever I failed to check off my to-do list the day before. Don't forget this, don't forget that; you promised to do thus and such but you didn't. Did that refund come through? Are we out of bread? More often I'm worrying in some completely neurotic way: what if, what if, what if? Or I'm berating myself about some failure. Or I'm ranting about the failures of others. There's something both exhausting and depressing about this incessant nagging and judging and obsessional ranting at three in the morning. I wish my inner radio station played the Brandenburg Concertos instead.

Pursued as nothing more than a stress-reduction technique, MBSR meditation teaches us not to listen to this broadcast. I'd be advised to shift my inner attention to the sensation of my own breathing—or to repeat "Brandenburg, Brandenburg, Brandenburg" or "Tennyson, Tennyson, Tennyson," or "fettuccine, fettuccine, fettuccine" to drown out the inner ranting. That works as far as it goes. In fact, it works remarkably well: that much has been rigorously documented. When I have been faithful to my daily body scans, I can fall back to sleep fairly quickly. That has been no small improvement in my quality of life.

Nonetheless, such techniques do not go very far.

Staying Alive . . .

To explain where MBSR meditation exercise does not get us, I want to begin by making an obvious observation. That All Talk All the Time radio station has a necessary function. It is reporting—All the Time—on my relationship to the world around me. Incessant judgmentalism, trivial though it is, reflects due diligence by sentient awareness. That is, keeping me alive requires monitoring my relationships to everything and to everyone around me. When it's functioning properly, in short, the That All Talk All the Time station is the brain doing its essential job: it is staying alert. It is trying to keep my body safe by alerting me—ceaselessly—to any potential threat.

Problems arise, however, when this primary, rudimentary, squirrelly awareness has sole command of the broadcast. We have extraordinarily more powerful cognitive abilities. If these more sophisticated skills are not engaged fruitfully, they will turn toxic. Primary consciousness will be corrupted into self-obsession.

At the heart of these more powerful cognitive abilities is our capacity to become self-aware.

Self-Awareness and the Moral Imagination

Self-awareness is the essential project of the human imagination: imagination is our ability to watch our own minds at work. Imagination is our ability to observe consciousness itself. As we watch ourselves observing, we become capable of noticing what we notice and furthermore noticing what we ignore as irrelevant.

As I said a minute ago: this rich and flexible self-awareness is essential to the highest creative achievement in any field. That's the case because being self-absorbed interferes with doing the best work. Worse yet, being unconsciously self-absorbed does more than interfere with creative problem solving. Unconscious egotists cannot imagine that they might be wrong. They cannot see any situation from someone else's point of view. They blind to their own egotism and, on the whole, massively invested in controlling others.

They are tiny totalitarians, constrained only by a lack of practical power. At least in my experience, they are also bitterly unhappy.

Christian teachings on prayer are centrally concerned with moving believers away from such unconscious egotism. As I said before: prayer in the Christian tradition is an introspective creative process designed to help us to develop a sensitive, flexible self-awareness. Prayer does so because Christianity regards unconscious self-absorption as morally dangerous. Unconscious egotism leads to equally unconscious projection, mindless hostility, intellectual rigidity, and so forth. It also leads to ignoring the needs of the needy: we can be willfully blind to others' suffering, willfully deaf to their cries for help. Unconscious egotism can also be paralyzing, as all of us have seen many times in life. As I have already explained, these are the moral conditions that Jesus' miracles address symbolically.

Prayer is designed to develop self-awareness because rich subjectivity is necessary for disciplined or morally mature objectivity: I can't keep myself out of it unless I have a firm, intelligent grip on that self. Such a grip is not repression. It is moral maturity.

For instance: compare Jonas Salk to Josef Mengele. Both were physicians. They were exact contemporaries. Both experimented on children. One developed the polio vaccine. The other is an icon of Nazi brutality. The difference between them is imagination, because imagination is necessarily prior to morality. Mengele's moral failures were predicated on a failure of imagination: he failed to see himself in those upon whom he experimented so brutally. He failed to recognize his own denial of common humanity with those who suffered under his hands. In biblical terms, he failed to love his neighbor as himself. The capacity to love our neighbor as ourselves presupposes, first and foremost, the imaginative and self-aware ability to see the neighbor as the self. People who profoundly lack that ability are defined as sociopaths.

Self-awareness can be strengthened by meditation because such exercise demonstrates to us that we are both the broadcaster and the audience of that All Talk All the Time radio station. As the audience, we can critique what is being broadcast.

But becoming a "critical listener," so to speak, is only the beginning. Barely the beginning. We are also the broadcaster. The more often petty egotism and self-obsession get "turned off," so to speak, the more likely it is that our most powerful cognitive skills will be liberated to perform their highest cognitive function.

What is that function? Synthesizing patterns. Creating and perceiving patterns. That's the key ability that philosophers call "imagination." That ability is what Einstein was pointing to when he said that imagination is more important that knowledge. He was not promoting fantasy over fact. He was arguing that patterns in the data are what matter.

Imagination and Wisdom

Imagination is crucial for achievement in any walk of life. But it has a massive religious function as well: imagination creates and perceives the patterns or relationships we call "wisdom." That's where Christian teachings about meditative prayer go far beyond MBSR meditation techniques. These teachings offer thousands of years of wisdom regarding these broadcasts. What do such broadcasts tell us about ourselves? About the lives we are living? What do they reveal about the world around us?

As historical theologian Roberta Bondi explores in *To Love as God Loves* (1987), in *Memories of God* (1995), and again in *In Ordinary Time* (1996), the density, complexity, and psychological sophistication of these ancient teachings can be quite remarkable. They can lead us from self-awareness to the moral question, Now what? Now what do I do about or with this insight into myself or into my own cultural context?

Christian meditation tradition also insists that as we become more adeptly or imaginatively self-aware, we will also become more aware of the presence of God. That awareness of God is the ultimate goal of all varieties of prayer. And God in turn is calling us—so to speak—to become ever more fully our authentic selves, not our blindly egotistical self-obsessed selves. This has been the core of my own religious experience.

William James, in *The Varieties of Religious Experience: A Study of Human Nature* (1902), cites many descriptions of the inward human encounter with sacred Presence. Over the years, I have come upon many more. As William James argued, they all do seem to say essentially the same thing. Such moments may all be an encounter with the same reality. Call it love, call it loving-kindness, call it compassion. Call it God. Or not. Name it however you want. The experience itself defies transcribing. Everyone says that too. What matters is not how we name it but whether we are loving, whether we are compassionate, whether we are kind. How we name this reality matters far less than how we live.

Any name is partial. Every name is incomplete. What can be said is but a shadow of the reality of the moment. The very name of God in Judeo-Christian tradition testifies to this. As I will explain in detail in *Confronting a Controlling God: Christian Humanism and the Moral Imagination*, chapters 8 and 9, the name of God is a promise of ongoing presence. Prayer in the Christian tradition is the effort to open our self-awareness widely enough to become aware of compassion as this ongoing and powerful Presence in our lives. Such love gives meaning and value to each of us. It reveals our immediate, intimate relationship to every other human being: we are all loved to this extent. It equally reveals how all that we behold around us—all of our natural and built environment—is also be-loved. And thus we are called into loving, responsible relationship with everything and everyone.

Imagination, Prayer, and Compassion

The goal of prayer, then, is allowing compassion to change our lives. As Blake notes in another context, "when it once is found / It renovates every Moment of the Day if rightly placed."[1] The goal of prayer, then, is allowing love to renovate our lives. The goal of prayer is allowing joy and meaning and generosity to lift what William Wordsworth called "the heavy and the weary weight / Of all

---

1. Blake, "Milton," plate 35, lines 44–45, in *The Poetry and Prose of William Blake*, 135.

this unintelligible world."[2] As we pray, the world becomes intelligible, both in its beauty and in its pain. The world becomes illuminated by a vision of what it should be or what it might become were each of us more fully conscious of how we are embraced by love and surrounded by beauty. Love is real, despite everything humanity has suffered, despite everything that has gone wrong, despite our inhumanity to one another.

Is prayer therapeutic in the sense that mindfulness-based stress reduction is therapeutic? You bet it is. But prayer also endeavors to go beyond reversing physiological stress responses to address the metaphysical problem of the human condition. We need to be loved. We need to be loving. We yearn for meaningful lives in a meaningful world.

And that's the artistic goal of the creative process that is prayer. The desire to lead such lives, and the practices that can help us to do so, are not fuzzy-minded magical thinking. Nor is any of it crazy. But prayer is a densely complex creative process, and so it is very easily misunderstood.

Or corrupted by those who want to get their hands on this process. More on that, of course, in *Confronting Religious Violence*, on the Christian heritage of theocracy and political violence.

2. Wordsworth, "Lines Written a Few Miles above Tintern Abbey," lines 39–40, in *Poetical Works*.

12

Other Ancient Prayer Practices

Before I conclude here, I have to say a few things about other varieties of prayer practice in the Christian tradition. Everybody knows that American Buddhists start out teaching people how to meditate. Despite the efforts of the World Community for Christian Meditation, it is not commonplace to find such instruction in a Christian congregation. The Christian practice of prayer and Christian teachings about prayer focus almost exclusively—or so it seems to me—on verbal prayer. Talky prayer. Praying with Scripture. Praying with the texts of inherited prayers. Working our way through lists of what we are supposed to say to God: praise, thanksgiving, supplication, and so forth. Meditation may be considered the purest prayer, the most powerful kind of prayer in Christian tradition—but most people meandering into the ordinary congregation would never be told that.

And so it behooves me, I've decided, to explain how these more common varieties of Christian prayer fit into my analysis of prayer as introspective creative process intended to foster both spiritual and personal growth. In this chapter I will look briefly at *lectio divina* (praying with Scripture) and spontaneous verbal prayer (putting your thoughts and feelings into sentences of your own composing—a.k.a. "talking to God.")

Praying with the Bible

Lectio divina (literally, holy reading) is a technique for praying with narratives. These are usually biblical narratives, although not necessarily. I remember my second-grade teacher leading us through a *lectio* exercise (second-grade style) on a story told about Jesus as a child in one of the many gospels that did not make the cut into the New Testament. This story made quite an impression on me, so I remembered it: Jesus was a kid once! Wow. What kind of kid was he? What was it like to play with him? Do you suppose he still remembers what it was like to be a kid? A kid like me? I was more impressed yet to realize, many decades later, that good Sister Virginia knew about these other gospels.

By analogy: *lectio divina* is something like an interactive video game played out in the mind's eye. Like any prayer, it is an exercise in openness to the ongoing presence of God. A scene is selected, and then within that scene a character is selected.

Then one imagines, as vividly as possible, the physical setting of the scene. One imagines feelings, the motives, and the physical experience of the chosen character, elaborating freely beyond the tautly minimalist style of scriptural storytelling. As I learned this exercise, one is free to play the part of God, or Jesus, or that enigmatic character, "the angel of the Lord." What did Jesus experience as he walked on the water? How did God feel when the Israelites made the golden calf while God and Moses were busy in meetings? Imaginatively entering the scene, one allows one's chosen character to do or to say whatever comes to mind, just as in an interactive video game. Then one watches what happens. How do other characters respond? One is free to play all the parts in turn, constrained only loosely by the plot structure of the original.

Anyone can imagine how happily the ordinary second-grade classroom might enter into such an exercise. After all, that's how we teach children to write short stories or poetry. Give them just a little to go on, and they will take off. But *lectio divina* is also a potent creative exercise for adults. It's a way to evoke spiritual insights that have been hovering on the edge of self-awareness.

In effect, *lectio divina* is an ancient, potent way of entering into the literary landscape of scriptural storytelling. Preachers do this all the time. They retell the story told in the Scriptures assigned for the day, elaborating it, opening up its metaphors, inviting the congregation to identify closely with some character—and then reflecting critically on the spiritual insight that follows from doing so. Such preaching can be brilliantly creative theologically. And it can be brutally, abusively manipulative—as we see, for instance, in Jonathan Edwards's infamous sermon, "Sinners in the Hands of an Angry God." It can be dangerous to pick a passage from Scripture, project your own unconscious stuff all over it, and then attribute the results to "God speaking to me."

Critical evaluation is a vitally important aspect of *lectio divina,* whether pursued in private or in small groups. Tradition insists that sharp, even skeptical reflection is crucial: we have an immense capacity to deceive ourselves. We have an equally immense ability to avoid facing what we need to face. The danger here, as any therapist might insist, is that the stories we elaborate for ourselves can reflect our problems and not our movement toward health. *Lectio divina* can be an invitation to post-traumatic nightmare fantasies. This danger is particularly acute for a naive believer under emotional stress in the midst of some crisis.

But it is equally true that *lectio divina* can be a spiritually challenging creative exercise to pursue under expert guidance and in a small group of trusted friends who will listen critically to what we might have to say afterwards about our own experience of the exercise. If we can claim the creative freedom to interact faithfully with the text, the stories we allow ourselves to imagine can be a movement of the soul toward greater health and integration. *Lectio divina* can be a way of listening deeply to the teachings Jesus offers in some of the Gospels. It can be a way of engaging symbolically with the symbolism of his miracles. Above all, *lectio divina* honestly and carefully pursued can be a way to realize that the Divine is always calling us toward our own deepest and most authentic selves.

"Conversation" with God

In the Christian tradition, prayer can also be imagined conversation with God. As with *lectio divina*, the potential for self-deception is enormous: all holy hell can be let loose by people thinking that God "told them" to do something.

This "conversation" model of prayer is quite a bit more common among Protestants than it is among Catholics, who rely much more centrally upon "set" prayers printed in books. Even where ancient safeguards are wisely kept in mind, Protestants talk about "talking to Jesus" in ways that I find startling. Perhaps that's because I grew up Catholic.

I was taught that after the ascension, Jesus of Nazareth went back to being the Second Person of the Trinity—an aspect of God's own self-awareness. What we deal with in prayer, I was taught, was not Jesus but the Spirit—and the etymological stem of "spirit" goes back to "breath" or to "wind." The Spirit is everywhere just as oxygen is everywhere; the Spirit is closer to us than our own inhale or exhale. But the Spirit, like the wind or the breath, cannot be visualized. There's nothing to see. And there is no one who speaks back. Feelings arise, of course. We are to attend to these feelings carefully, because they might be genuine responses to the Presence of God. But they are our own feelings.

That's how I was taught. Or that's what I heard and remembered of what I was taught, which is of course potentially quite different. Others were taught differently; they have memories very different from mine. They were taught to think about their inward awareness of what I've been calling divine Presence as the specific presence of Jesus himself, the man from Nazareth, immediately present to them in spiritual form. As a result, for them prayer is "talking to Jesus."

I still find such teachings disconcerting. Perhaps that's not unlike encountering what looks like beef stew or shepherd's pie seasoned with anything other than bacon fat and onions and a splash of Worcestershire. It may taste very good. It may be welcome and filling on a cold night. The people who eat this way are good and sane people, reliable friends, high-functioning professionals. They are not crazies hearing voices telling them to do irresponsible things. But at some stubborn level of my heart, this "talking to Jesus" business will remain something like beef stew seasoned with rosemary and tarragon. The only thing more disconcerting is oatmeal made with water not milk, or perhaps scrambled eggs with curry powder. Yes, good people eat this way. Lots of them. I don't.

Or at least not usually. Such "conversational" prayer did arise in me spontaneously at one point in my life. I found that quite distressing. It is not an experience I seek or invite. But many people do—many rock-solid sane and spiritually wise people. I defer to them on the topic.

The obvious risk behind "conversational" models of prayer is fully—even sternly—recognized within prayer teachings in the Christian tradition. What Christian tradition calls "the discernment of spirits" reflects a remarkably sophisticated appreciation of the power of the unconscious. There is a big difference between incipient schizophrenia and genuine creative insight.

Contemporary psychotherapy, in fact, arose as the Victorian secularizing of traditions thousands of years old regarding "the care of the soul." The so-called "therapeutic relationship"—the patient's encounter with a loving, wise, reliable, honest, shrewd but nonjudgmental therapist—is transparently modeled upon religious accounts of relationship with God as mediated through this conversational prayer technique. In conversation-prayer with God, so to speak, I can say absolutely anything and I will be understood. I will be accepted. I will be neither judged nor condemned. Nor will my egotism be indulged. But the challenges from God that I encounter in such prayer will never be more than I can handle without disintegrating.

To distinguish between the Sacred and individual unconscious stuff, the spiritual seeker may need help. Such supportive structure can come from the vast array of spiritual teachings in the tradition. It can come from religious friends, from books, from local clergy, from the experience of communal worship. Help can also be available from professional caregivers called spiritual companions or spiritual directors. There are both national and local training programs for them, mostly in some affiliation with the Roman Catholic church; standards vary. It is wise to be cautious, just as one would be in seeking secular psychotherapy.

The Difficulty of Honest Conversation

Ann Ulanov, a Jungian therapist, and Barry Ulanov, a professor of English, collaborated on the best guide to verbal prayer that I have ever read: *Primary Speech: A Psychology of Prayer* (1982). Their arguments suggest that I've been missing out on something: it can be a remarkable challenge, they explain, to articulate to ourselves exactly what we are feeling or fearing or what we yearn for, particularly in the Presence of a sympathetic listener who knows the truth about us and the truth about our situation from the outset and without being told. I've read their book repeatedly, wrestling each time.

The Ulanovs begin with what I've been calling my All Talk All the Time radio station. This incessant verbal flow is what they call "primary speech" in their book of that title. These broadcasts, they caution, reveal our deepest identity, our fiercest needs, our most potent fears. Maybe we complain that we can't shut down this radio station—but the fact is that we don't listen to it attentively either. We don't want to listen critically to this primary self-talk because self-knowledge can be both costly and dangerous.

And so, they argue, prayer begins in listening attentively to this verbal flow of yearnings and fears. Never mind the mantra and the endless re-centering of attention on the breath. Sit still awhile, listening carefully to the broadcast. Take notes. What is being said? Did you know you felt that, or thought that, or feared that, or wanted that?

We should listen like this, they argue, because opening ourselves to full awareness of our own yearnings and fears also opens us to the transforming of these desires and fears. Such transformation happens in prayer if we bring our desires and fears into the presence of God, in effect telling God what we want, what terrifies us, what we are worried about, and so forth. Facing what we fear, facing what we desire—that is what ordinary psychotherapy involves, does it not? Yes, some people desperately need the support of a therapist to do this. But not everyone. Furthermore, Christian spiritual teachings can offer some of the same support that therapists offer. And more: faith involves the belief that love is the ultimate cosmic power. Faith involves the conviction that we are deeply loved and fully accepted by God exactly as we are. Faith is the confidence that with God's help deep personal change is possible.

The process of articulating our desires, the Ulanovs argue, gradually and naturally shifts our desires. They change and enlarge. What might have begun simply in greed or vanity or neurotic self-absorption slowly gives way to a desire genuinely to understand ourselves, to see ourselves whole, know firsthand what is the case about life. That's an assumption on their part, obviously. But it is an assumption based upon years of experience in providing spiritual guidance.

Yes, we might indeed begin by sending tech support messages to God the Engineer Almighty. But over time the futility of that becomes clear. The inadequacy of Engineer Almighty theology becomes undeniable. What then? We begin with these images of who we need God to be, they explain—we begin with our naive, straightforward projections of control needs and so forth—because over time we will come to recognize that these are in fact projections. The images are not God.

One of the first tasks in prayer, they caution, is to become aware of the many different images of God that surface within us, questioning the origins of these images, questioning their validity, and so forth. Our images for God need to be something we talk about with God as we pray—so to speak—something we interrogate closely as part of the prayer itself. In this way (and perhaps with ongoing help from someone like Ann Ulanov, professionally trained therapist and theologically sophisticated spiritual guide) we will slowly recognize that these images are all versions of a private idolatry.

Over a longer time yet, we will gradually withdraw our energies from any particular image for God. We will also withdraw from any theological position about the nature of God. As the Jews cautioned, any image at all for God is far "less" that what God is, and any propositional claim about God risks blasphemy. Even saying

"God is love" is saying both too much and too little. It's the idolatrous or blasphemous substitute of a concept for the elusive reality hovering at the far edges of self-awareness, something felt not seen, and even at that not in the physical senses. Laurence Freeman, the Benedictine monk I referred to earlier, insists that one consequence of sustained meditation practice as a prayer discipline is that one distinctly loses interest in "the supernatural" as a metaphysical category and a problem in epistemology.

As the Ulanovs' work makes clear, there are dense intersections between spiritual counsel based on the client's prayer life and classic psychotherapy. These intersections have been substantively explored: the literature on this topic is immense. If you would like to know more, good starting points in the Jungian tradition are Janice Brewi and Anne Brennan, *Mid-life Psychological and Spiritual Perspectives* (2004) or their earlier book, *Mid-life Spirituality and Jungian Archetypes* (1999). I have also long admired the work of Gerald May, whose career involved work both as a psychiatrist and as a spiritual mentor. He is particularly fascinating on the difference between the two. I'd particularly recommend *Care of Mind, Care of Spirit* (1982), although I also deeply enjoyed *The Awakened Heart: Living Beyond Addiction* (1991).

Those not struggling with deep-seated psychological conflicts might prefer to approach the experience of prayer through the Celtic tradition. The folk-poem prayers of the Celtic tradition are psychologically nuanced. They have a warm, confident view of human nature. The Celtic traditions sees us as healthy and moving toward greater health amidst the ordinary difficulties of our lives. "Sin" is not a obsession. Nor are we portrayed as riven by the deep inner conflicts and psychic anguish presupposed by the German romantic tradition behind both Freud and Jung. On the Celtic tradition I recommend Esther de Waal, both *The Celtic Way of Prayer* (1997) and *Every Earthly Blessing: Recovering the Celtic Tradition* (1999). Also on my short list of "not to be missed" spiritual guides is J. Philip Newell, particularly *Listening for the Heartbeat of God: A Celtic Spirituality* (1997) and *Christ of the Celts: The Healing of Creation* (2008). Newell has also composed two short, beautifully illustrated guides to daily prayer, *Celtic Benediction: Morning and Night*

Prayer (2000) and *Sounds of the Eternal: A Celtic Psalter* (2002), which also has a week's worth of morning and nighttime prayers. One or the other of these two prayer books has been next to my favorite armchair since they were first published. I've given away many copies over the years. As the Anglicans are famous for saying, how we pray is what we believe theologically: Newell's prayers get it right.

Or so it seems to me. Prayer is intensely, vulnerably personal.

Praying for Others; Praying for Enemies

Praying for others is one of the most complex and most often misunderstood aspects of verbal prayer. It is not asking for magical intervention. Praying for enemies in particular strikes many people as impossible if not obscene. But its point is to help us withdraw from fantasies of violent revenge. Its point is to release us from the bitter prison of our own anguish and outrage.

We pray for our enemies in an effort to limit the damage they have caused to us. We are not praying for them because we want for them what they want for themselves. We are praying for them because their actions have demonstrated to us how far they are from the transformative love that God is or that God offers. They are lost; they are broken. Our prayers won't change that—prayer does not change outcomes. But prayer for our enemies can help to free us from the toxicity of hating those who hate us. If we feel hated or despised or discriminated against (which can be a perfectly accurate assessment), our lives can be swamped by the toxicity of despising those who despise us.

Our prayers for them can also help to keep us from demonizing them—and thus giving way to the demonic in ourselves—even as it reassures us that there are much bigger truths and much greater realities than whatever has just happened. But here's a key caution: one can attempt to pray for enemies only amidst a pre-existing practice of prayer. Nobody begins a prayer practice by praying for enemies. That would be a most serious mistake.

We are more likely to start by praying for someone we love who faces some sort of difficulty. Even robust nonbelievers can find themselves praying such prayers, whether wordlessly or with words. What is going on there? Is that a primitive recourse to magical thinking?

In praying for others, I face the depth of my concern for them. That includes the depth of my own anxiety on their behalf—an anxiety that probably reveals my own deepest fears about my own life, my own deepest anger, my own deepest and least conscious grief. I imagine now that this is part of what Mrs. O'Malley was doing when she made that novena for me my senior year in college.

In 1971, tensions between her generation and my generation were immense. My generation was in full-throated rebellion against gender stereotypes and the usual gender roles. Our mothers' generation often experienced this as a wholesale rejection of their lives, their values, and above all their sacrifices for their families. As a generation, they felt spurned and betrayed by their daughters. And we felt rejected and betrayed by our mothers.

On the other hand, I'm sure my mother's generation was also wracked by ambivalence about what their daughters were daring to do: we had opportunities most of them never dreamed of having. A few women had fought to open doors, and now a whole generation of us were storming through. Of course our mothers were ambivalent. My own mother grieved her whole life that she never had a chance to go to college—and now to have a daughter become a college professor? Contemplating that possibility might have been painful beyond words. The ambivalence of our mothers was matched, of course, by our own self-doubts. What a toxic brew! What could have been more appropriate than a novena to the patron saint of hopeless causes?

Mrs. O'Malley had to be facing all that. Facing into it squarely, with an uncommon spiritual courage. She undoubtedly knew how distraught my parents were when I said I wanted to get a doctorate rather than settling down immediately and producing the grandchildren for which they yearned. Mrs. O'Malley's novena was something like a spiritual invitation from her that I should face all this conflict in the presence of God as encountered in prayer. She was insisting that God meets us amidst all of our deepest fears. We need to trust that loving Presence and to seek it in prayer. As teachings go, that's bedrock. Such recourse to prayer was commonplace in the world she and I shared.

The reality of our own fears for ourselves is always a fact to be faced in prayer ostensibly "for" someone else. As anyone who has faced real troubles will tell you, it is not helpful when a friend shows up awash in his or her own anxiety over what's going on. My sister calls that "the two problems problem." If some people discover you have a problem, then you have two problems.

In my experience, praying for others strengthens my solidarity with them and my compassion for them. Above all, it prepares me to be genuinely, quietly present to them in their pain—undeterred, unfrazzled, unafraid of what they are going through, not trying to fix it for them, which is of course my default setting. I am at least less taut than I would have been if I had *not* prayed. Prayer can helps me to be focused enough to recognize and organize myself to do whatever might be genuinely helpful.

Often, of course, the only genuinely helpful thing we can do is to be quietly, intensely, courageously present to them amidst their pain. At least for me, praying for someone clarifies the difference between my being genuinely helpful and my simply doing something—anything—to alleviate my own anxiety about their situation. I don't have to know what to say, I've realized. I don't have to know what to do. I just have to show up, eyes open and mouth closed. Praying can help me do that.

Among believers, the knowledge that others are praying for you is deeply supportive. It counteracts the isolation experienced by those who are suffering. My prayers for you—or yours for me—are, in effect, a gutsy effort to imagine our ways deeply into someone else's suffering. And then we sit with the reality of that pain, inhaling and exhaling, until we also find a way to be open to the transcendent source of the requisite love and courage.

This is not easy. It is not easy at all. It all sounds so rosy. It's not. Praying for those in real pain, like praying for our enemies, is very dicey stuff. I think that's why it's so often performed so badly in public settings: the intimate vulnerabilities are immense.

Does praying for others change outcomes? No. Every book on prayer that I have ever read always cautions, "do not pray for outcomes." God is not a vending machine: do not pray for changes in the physical world. Pray for comfort, for resilience, for good judgment, for confidence, for courage, for emotional and psychological healing, for the wherewithal to remember that God is present no matter what. But do not pray for changes in the material world. Do not pray for a biopsy outcome unless you are so overwhelmed by your own anxiety that all you can say is "don't let it be malignant, don't let it be malignant" over and over again until you have emptied that well of wordy anxiety. At the bottom of that well, at the rock-solid bottom of the bottom of the abyss, there is not nothing. There are something like hands, doing something like cradling us as we might cradle a fluffy chick. There is Presence.

Does prayer help? Well, what do you mean by "help"? How is "help" to be measured? Loneliness hurts. Those who suffer acutely almost always feel acutely lonely. Most of us are plainly afraid of anyone in acute pain. We back away. But praying for someone who is suffering draws us close again. We work through our own issues so that we can stand by them resolutely as they face theirs.

In praying for others about a problem they are facing, I am, in the end, praying for myself. As the Ulanovs explain, I am talking to myself as a way of directing my own feelings and my own spiritual awareness. I do so to express my own anxieties and thereby face them more squarely. I do so in hopes of responding appropriately no matter what outcome my friends might face. I do so because I need to rustle up all the resilience and good grace available to my inherently reactive soul. I need resilience and grace if I'm going to be of any use at all amidst their crisis: they probably don't need me swooping in to take control. I need to be a source of strength for my friends, not one of the additional problems with which they have to cope. I need resilience and grace in order to focus on *their* needs, not my own.

Such prayer is not magical thinking. It's not "talking to yourself" in any crazy-person way. Deep compassion—by whatever name—is one of the most potent forces shaping our lives. There is a level of reality at which love does indeed make the world go round. That's not geology. Nor is it astrophysics.

It's faith. It's not for the timid, the fuzzy minded, or the naive. It will never be rendered obsolete by scientific achievements, no matter how revolutionary, nor by engineering prowess, no matter how dazzling. It may not be for everyone, but that's okay. Neither is playing the violin.

13

Confronting Fundamentalism: Where Does This Leave Us?

Christianity properly understood can best collaborate with empirical science properly understood if all the people involved on all sides understand and resist the ways in which each has been misappropriated into opposing the other. Christianity is not a failed effort at doing what empirical science does. Empirical science is not a rival religion determined to eradicate Christianity. These misunderstandings both derive from the Western cultural desperation to reestablish an ideological foundation for the unquestionable authority once wielded by our divine-right monarchs and ancient emperors. To our collective horror, we found that unquestionable authority is secular form. It showed up as twentieth-century totalitarianism.

At our collective best, however, both Christianity and empirical science forthrightly acknowledge the human capacity for error. Both groups forthrightly acknowledge our need to collaborate and our capacity wisely to call one another's errors into account. Whether you call failures "sin" or whether you call failures "results that cannot be replicated," both groups know that to be human is to be fallible. And we know, in our various ways, how vitally important it is to encourage in one another the best that is in us.

It will take the best that is in us—the best in all of us, whether we are believers or not, whether we are scientists or whether we are merely citizens—to bring the best of empirical work to bear in creating a viable, vital future for all of humanity on this small and increasingly fragile planet.

Works Cited

Begley, Sharon. *Train Your Mind, Change Your Brain: How a New Science Reveals Our Extraordinary Potential to Transform Ourselves.* New York: Ballantine, 2008.

Benson, Herbert, with Miriam Z. Klipper. *The Relaxation Response.* New York: Avon, 1975.

Blake, William. *The Poetry and Prose of William Blake.* Edited by David V. Erdman. New York: Doubleday, 1970.

Bondi, Roberta. *In Ordinary Time: Healing the Wounds of the Heart.* Nashville, TN: Abingdon, 1996.

———. *Memories of God: Theological Reflections on a Life.* Nashville, TN: Abingdon, 1995.

———. *To Love as God Loves: Conversations With the Early Church.* Philadelphia: Fortress, 1987.

Brewi, Janice, and Anne Brennan. *Mid-Life Psychological and Spiritual Perspectives.* Berwick, ME: Nicolas-Hays, 2004.

———. *Mid-Life Spirituality and Jungian Archetypes.* York Beach, ME: Nicholas-Hays, 1999.

Brock, Rita Nakashima, and Ruth Ann Parker. *Saving Paradise: How Christianity Traded Love of This World for Crucifixion and Empire.* Boston: Beacon, 2008.

Crosby, Alfred W. *The Measure of Reality: Quantification and Western Society, 1250–1600.* Cambridge: Cambridge University Press, 1997.

Dalai Lama, *Beyond Religion: Ethics for the Whole World.* New York: Houghton Mifflin Harcourt, 2011

———. *The Good Heart: A Buddhist Perspective on the Teachings of Jesus.* Boston: Wisdom, 1996.

———. *Toward a True Kinship of Faiths: How the World's Religions Can Come Together.* New York: Doubleday, 2010.

Davidson, Richard J., with Sharon Begley. *The Emotional Life of Your Brain.* New York: Hudson Street, 2012.

Dennett, Daniel. *Freedom Evolves.* New York: Viking, 2003

De Waal, Esther. *The Celtic Way of Prayer.* New York: Doubleday, 1997.

————. *Every Earthly Blessing: Rediscovering the Celtic Tradition*. Harrisburg, PA: Morehouse, 1999.

De Waal, Frans. *Primates and Philosophers: How Morality Evolves*. Princeton: Princeton University Press, 2006.

Dupré, John. *Human Nature and the Limits of Science*. Oxford: Clarendon, 2001.

Eagleton, Terry. *Reason, Faith, & Revolution: Reflections on the God Debate*. New Haven, CT: Yale University Press, 200

Epstein, Greg M. *Good Without God: What a Billion Nonreligious People Do Believe*. New York: Morrow, 2009.

Freeman, Laurence. *Jesus the Teacher Within*. New York: Continuum, 2000.

Geertz, Clifford. "Religion as a Cultural System." In *Anthropological Approaches to the Study of Religion*," edited by Michael Banton, 1–46. London: Tavistock, 1966.

Hart, David Bentley. *Atheist Delusions: The Christian Revolution and Its Fashionable Enemies*. New Haven, CT: Yale University Press, 2009.

Heyrman, Christine Leigh. *Southern Cross: The Beginnings of the Bible Belt*. New York: Knopf, 1997.

Hollinger, David A. *After Cloven Tongues of Fire: Protestant Liberalism in Modern American History*. Princeton, NJ: Princeton University Press, 2013.

Hyde, Lewis. *The Gift: Creativity and the Artist in the Modern World*. New York: Vintage, 2007.

James, William, *The Varieties of Religious Experience: A Study in Human Nature*. 1902; rpt. edited by Martin E. Marty, New York: Penguin, 1982.

Kearney, Richard. *Anatheism: Returning to God After God*. New York: Columbia University Press, 2010.

Lippmann, Walter. *A Preface to Morals*. New York: Macmillan, 1929.

Luhrman, T. M. *When God Talks Back: Understanding the American Evangelical Relationship to God*. New York: Knopf, 2012.

Martin, William. *With God on Our Side: The Rise of the Religious Right in America*. New York: Broadway, 2005.

May, Gerald G. *The Awakened Heart: Living Beyond Addiction*. San Francisco: HarperSanFrancisco, 1991.

————. *Will and Spirit*. 1982; rpt. San Francisco: HarperSanFrancisco, 1987

Midgley, Mary. *Evolution as a Religion: Strange Hopes and Stranger Fears*. Rev. ed. New York: Routledge, 2002.

Myers, Ched. *Binding the Strong Man: A Political Reading of Mark's Story of Jesus*. Maryknoll NY: Orbis, 1988.

Myers, Ched, and Matthew Colwell. *Our God is Undocumented: Biblical Faith and Immigrant Justice*. Maryknoll NY: Orbis, 2012.

Newell, J. Philip. *Celtic Benediction: Morning and Night Prayer*. Grand Rapids MI: Eerdmans, 2000

————. *Christ of the Celts: The Healing of Creation*. San Francisco: Jossey-Bass, 2008.

————. *Listening for the Heartbeat of God: A Celtic Spirituality.* New York: Paulist, 1997.

————. *Sounds of the Eternal: A Celtic Psalter Morning and Night Prayer.* Grand Rapids, MI: Eerdmans, 2002.

Pattison, George. *Anxious Angels: A Retrospective View of Religious Existentialism.* New York: St. Martin's, 1999.

Sacks, Jonathan. *The Dignity of Difference: How to Avoid the Clash of Civilizations.* New York: Continuum, 2002.

Steindl-Rast, David. *Gratefulness, the Heart of Prayer: An Approach to Life in Fullness.* New York: Paulist, 1984.

Taylor, Charles. *A Secular Age.* Cambridge, MA: Belknap Press of Harvard University Press, 2007.

Thoreau, Henry David. *Walden and Civil Disobedience.* Norton Critical Edition. Ed Owen Thomas. New York: Norton, 1966.

Tylor, Edward. *Primitive Culture.* London: Murray, 1871.

Ulanov, Ann, and Barry Ulanov. *Primary Speech: A Psychology of Prayer.* Atlanta: Knox, 1982.

Underhill, Evelyn. *Mysticism: A Study in the Nature and Development of Man's Spiritual Consciousness.* New York: New American, 1974.

Wallace, Catherine M. *Selling Ourselves Short: Why We Struggle to Earn a Living and Have a Life.* Grand Rapids, MI: Brazos, 2003.

Wilkinson, Richard, and Kate Pickett. *The Spirit Level: Why Greater Equality Makes Societies Stronger.* New York: Bloomsbury, 2009.

Wilson, David Sloan. *Darwin's Cathedral: Evolution, Religion, and the Nature of Society.* Chicago: University of Chicago Press, 2002

Wilson, A. N. *God's Funeral: A Biography of Faith and Doubt in Western Civilization.* New York: Ballantine, 1999.

Wordsworth, William. *Poetical Works.* Edited by Thomas Hutchinson; rev. ed. edited by Ernest De Selincourt. New York: Oxford University Press, 1910.

Zuckerman, Phil. *Faith No More: Why People Reject Religion.* New York: Oxford University Press, 2012.